SUCCEEDING IN BUSINESS

Starting and running a practice for
professionals in therapy
and healthcare

Published by Holistic Therapy Books
3 Ness Road, Burwell, Cambridge. CB5 0AA
© 2003 Holistic Therapy Books

First edition May 2003
Updated and reprinted November 2004

ISBN 1-903348-05-6

ACKNOWLEDGEMENTS

This book was written by Pip Hardy and Tony Sumner of Pilgrim Projects, Cambridge with considerable help from Margaret Alexander, Sheila White, and Hugh Hillyard-Parker.

The text and cover were designed by Pip Blakemore of Design Study, Mundford, Norfolk, and laid out by Andy Wilson of The Write Idea, Cambridge.

We are grateful to the following for reading and commenting on the manuscript of this book:

Jamie Drake, Hair stylist, Reeds Hair, Cambridge

Frances Fewell, BA, Cert Ed. BRCP (Aroma Advisor); Senior Lecturer and Pathway Leader for the BSc (Hons) Complementary Medicine, Anglia Polytechnic University

Stephan John, BA(Hons), MA(Ed), PGCE; Education Development Manager, Small Firms Enterprise Development Initiative

Laurence Noone, BA (Hons), ACA

Julie Smith, BA (Hons), RSHom, Joint Course Leader (Homeopathy), Department of Complementary Therapies, School of Integrated Health, University of Westminster

Judith Tillson, Barrister (non-practising); BA (Hons), Lecturer in Law and Programme Leader HNC Business, Cambridge Regional College

Maria Wray, ITEC, MGPBT

PHOTOGRAPHIC CREDITS

Vicky Guntun, Mad Hatters Hair and Beauty, Cambridge

Jenny Chin's Dental Surgery, Cambridge

Beatrix Veal and Bob Blair, Arjuna Health Centre, Cambridge

Alison Judge, Amanda Ody, Ashley Scott, James Dowle and Lisa Barnwell, Napiers Herbal Health Care, Cambridge

James Robertson, Kei Masuda and Matt Martinez, The Glassworks, Cambridge

Ede and Ravenscroft Ltd, Cambridge

CONTENTS

INTRODUCTION

This book is intended as a guide to setting up and running a successful small business. While the book covers the ITEC syllabus for the modules on Business Awareness and Professional Conduct it will be useful to students of any of the main qualifications requiring an understanding of business and professional practice. *Succeeding in Business* provides practical help through the early stages of setting up and running a small business. Complementary therapists, other healthcare professionals and people working in beauty or sports therapy will find the book particularly relevant.

Quotations and case studies from real people help to highlight the joys and challenges of running a small business. Topics covered include:

* setting up and running the business

* relationships, professionalism and ethics

* the environment (including legislation and regulation)

* business development and marketing

and a helpful list of resources.

ABOUT THIS BOOK

So you are thinking of running your own small business? You may be looking forward enthusiastically to running an enjoyable and rewarding business, but you may also be nervous about the prospect. There is a lot to think about and plenty to do.

'I was very anxious about setting up on my own. I went out to lunch with a friend who had been a freelance editor for several years. She commented that it was a bit like diving off a high diving board – terrifying from the top, but once you've made the decision to jump, it's exhilarating and then, once you're in the water, as long as you can swim, everything will be fine.'

Lissia, Alexander Technique Teacher

You don't have to do everything yourself – there are plenty of people who can give you advice and help you make a success of your business, especially in the early days. This book will point you in the right direction.

Make sure there really is a market for your idea/product/service, and that you have the necessary skills and knowledge to make a success of it.

'Wherever you see a successful business, someone once made a courageous decision.'

Peter Drucker

Who is this book for?

This book is for anyone thinking of setting up in business, but is especially relevant if you are a:

- complementary therapist
- beauty therapist
- sports therapist
- physiotherapist or occupational therapist
- health care professional (working inside or outside the health service)
- manager of a residential care home
- hairdresser
- counsellor or psychotherapist.

'This is a family-run business – we've been here for 12 years now. My parents, my two sisters and my partner all work for the business. I work six days a week but I wouldn't have it any other way. I'm my own boss and I know I can rely on the people I work with.'

Donna, owner of a beauty salon

You have probably decided on your career because you like people and want to help them feel healthier, happier, fitter, more beautiful, or whatever. You will want to concentrate on practising your skills and not necessarily on the business side of things.

'I've spent ages training as an aromatherapist and I love the feeling of making people feel relaxed and happy. If I had wanted to run a business, I would have become an accountant.'

Jody, aromatherapist

However well-trained and experienced you may be in your particular line of work, in order to run a successful business, you need to acquire a whole new set of skills and learn to view the world of work in a different way.

Did you know…?

2.6 million businesses trading in the UK at the beginning of 2001 were sole traders and partnerships.

Small businesses account for 99% of all businesses in the UK.

Between 1995 and 2000 most of the growth in the business population has been in the number of 'micro' businesses employing fewer than ten people, and in the number of one-person companies.

Statistics from the DTI Small Business Service www.sbs.gov.uk

---

Small businesses like yours are essential to the economy. Many small businesses begin as the result of a brilliant idea, but without the skills and knowledge necessary to bring the idea to fruition.

How this book can help you

One of the chief causes of the high failure rate of new businesses is lack of preparation and attention to the practical tasks involved in setting up in business. This book aims to give you the skills to manage the range of tasks involved – and so become one of the thousands of people who are successful in their business. It will guide you through the process of setting up and getting started in business. It will help you avoid some of the pitfalls and make more of the pleasures of running a successful small business, and ensure that you work ethically, professionally and successfully.

'Oh I don't think I want to set up my own business. Well, I suppose sometime in the future I might consider it but I would never do it on my own – I would want to do it in partnership with someone else. It's a lot of work though – the manager here works evenings and weekends and you're always having to worry about money. I don't want all that hassle – I want to cut hair!'

Jamie, 21 year-old hairdresser

HOW TO USE THIS BOOK

The book is divided into an introductory skills check, four main sections and a resources section. Each section focuses on a particular aspect of starting or managing a small business. The sections are broken down into topics so you can easily cover a subject in a short time.

There are a number of activities and checklists to encourage you to think about what you have to do and, in some cases, what you have already done. You may find it helpful to make notes in the book itself about particular issues that relate to your business.

'Success is the sum of small efforts, repeated day in and day out.'

Robert Collier

Skills checks

There are five skills checks, one for each section of the book. They will help you see what you already know, what you need to find out and where to go in the book to find out about specific topics.

Take some time to look at each skills check in turn. Think about each issue and put a tick in the box to show whether you think you know everything that you need to know about a topic, or whether you and your business could do with understanding a little more, or benefit from a little help.

Be honest with yourself! If you are not sure about a topic, have a quick look at the information within it to see whether you would benefit from reading it in more detail.

Of course, you may prefer to start at the beginning and work your way through the whole book. The important thing is to use the book in the way that suits you and your business best. When you have finished the book, you may like to come back to these pages so that you can see how much progress you have made.

> Did **you know…?**
>
> 85% of small businesses fail in their first year.

Overview of the five sections

The first two sections look at the issues that arise when you decide to set up and run a business of your own. Section 1 covers the business side of things, including many of the practical steps you need to take, while Section 2 looks at how to practise in a professional and successful manner, building good and, we hope, profitable relationships with clients, suppliers and professional colleagues.

Sections 3 and 4 will help you to manage the environmental maze of legal, ethical, financial and practical issues that you will have to deal with in the course of your career.

The final section summarises where you can find useful resources and help in running your business – websites, government departments, colleges, and professional and business support organisations.

Skills checks

Skills check for Section 1: Setting up and running the business

Setting up business as, say, a complementary therapist, masseur or hairdresser isn't like buying a squeegee, bucket and baseball cap and hanging around at traffic lights to clean car windows. You've got to sort out bank accounts, tax, National Insurance and even premises. Run through this skills check to spot those tricky little issues like insurance…

Do you know about:		Page	Topic	Know it all already!	Somebody help me!
1	Where you will work				
2	Working from home				
3	Finding premises				
4	Different forms of business				
5	Tax, National Insurance and VAT				
6	Accounts				
7	Keeping the books				
8	Budgeting and planning				
9	Communication technology				
10	Information technology				
11	Legal issues and insurance				
12	Finding and keeping staff				
13	Keeping and storing records				

Skills check for Section 2: Relationships, professionalism and ethics

'I didn't start my own business just to do an average job averagely.'

'We started our business to do a job we enjoy in a way that clients and fellow professionals respect and admire.'

'We want other people to recommend us because we do a good job in a professional manner.'

Run through the following skills check to identify areas that you think you could do with polishing up.

Do you know about:	Page	Topic	Know it all already!	Somebody help me!
1 Being professional: preparing yourself and your surroundings				
2 Providing a professional service				
3 Keeping up to date (continuing professional development)				
4 Being a reflective practitioner				
5 Being an ethical practitioner				
6 Confidentiality and consent				
7 Good relationships – introduction				
8 Working with other therapists				
9 Working with the medical profession				
10 Contraindications and danger signals				
11 Communicating with clients – introduction				
12 Communicating with clients – listening skills				
13 Communicating with clients – body language				
14 Communicating with clients – receiving negative feedback				
15 Working with clients – the first contact				
16 Working with clients – managing expectations				

Skills check for Section 3: The environment

Factors in your working environment that affect you every day range from legislation, like the Health and Safety at Work Act, to the commercial issue of what to do about a bounced cheque. This skills check will alert you to any areas that you could do with looking at.

Do you know about:	Page	Topic	Know it all already!	Somebody help me!
1 Legislation governing health and safety at work				
2 Legislation governing employing staff				
3 Legislation governing data protection and equal opportunities				
4 Legislation governing professional membership and licensing				
5 First aid				
6 Fire safety				
7 Infections and hygiene				
8 Sterilisation and waste disposal				
9 Security				
10 Stock control				
11 Managing reception and appointments				
12 Dealing with difficulties				

Skills check for Section 4: Business development and marketing

Even when you've got yourself up and running in your business, there are always those nagging worries about where the next client is going to come from, how much to charge, and whether it's all worth it. This skills check will help you to find topics that cover ways to develop and promote you business. Think about your answers and be honest.

Do you know about:	Page	Topic	Know it all already!	Somebody help me!
Marketing				
Promotion				
Selling				
Preparing a presentation				
Giving a presentation				

Skills check for Section 5: Resources

Try this skills check if you don't know where to find help or support from colleagues in similar professions, would like to read more on a particular topic, or need to look at examples of letters and forms.

Do you know about:	Page	Topic	Know it all already!	Somebody help me!
Code of Practice				
Sample forms and letters				
Books, websites, addresses and other resources				
How to find something in this book				

Okay – where to now? Well, take a look back at your skills checks, and move on to the topics that you have singled out for further attention.

Section 1

Setting up and running
the business

Topic 1 Where will you work?

One of the first things you need to think about is where you will work. You and your clients will be spending many hours in this place, so it is important to make sure that it is a pleasant place to be, as well as being suitable for your work – somewhere where you, your clients and staff can enjoy spending time.

This topic, and the next two, cover the things you will need to think about when making the important decision of where to work.

FACTORS TO CONSIDER

Your working environment both influences and is influenced by you. With careful planning, it can be a pleasant and calm place, where both you and your clients will feel relaxed and comfortable.

Many people decide to work from home – at least to begin with – because it is cheaper and more convenient. It can also fit in well with family commitments. Many other people choose to work in a clinic, salon or therapy centre, often alongside other people doing similar kinds of work.

You may be drawn either to work from home or to work in a clinic or salon, but try to keep an open mind until you have considered everything. When you examine the pros and cons, you may find that one option has clear practical advantages over the other. You may find that your first choice isn't the best one.

Remember that your first decision is not irrevocable – you can always change your mind later. The next topic looks in more detail at working from home, while Topic 3 focuses on finding premises.

Checklist: Thinking about where to work

Ideally, what size space would you like to work in?

What amenities would you like to have available for your clients?

What image do you wish to project – businesslike, professional, informal, welcoming, cutting-edge, alternative?

Do you like to work with other professionals around you, or on your own?

Do you like to travel to work, and then leave it physically behind you at the end of the day?

Do you like being out and about?

Do you prefer working flexible, rather than office, hours and being within easy reach of schools, etc.?

Do you want a local client base?

FIRST THINGS TO THINK ABOUT

Let's begin with the ideal – you can bring in the restrictions later. What would be your perfect workplace? What do you offer and what is unique about it? Consider the factors in the following checklist. You might find it useful to make notes about each of them.

Now consider what factors might affect your choice, for instance:

- ease of access to clients – can they find you easily; will they have restricted mobility, vision, hearing; is there easy parking?
- suitability of location for generating business
- what is affordable
- travel time and costs
- communications (telephone, fax, Internet, etc.) – are these available or can they be installed?
- domestic responsibilities
- suppliers and services – (clean towels, deliveries of stock and stationery) is there easy access?
- planning or other restrictions
- size and suitability of working space
- whether you will be working full- or part-time
- the image you want to present
- possible government or local authority assistance, if you live in an area which has initiatives aimed at stimulating new business
- possible restrictions, e.g. planning, change of use, etc.
- any legal restrictions, for example, on working from home.

DRAWING UP A PLAN

Take some time now to sketch out a plan of your work space. If you have considered what you definitely need, you will be in a better position to make wise decisions about where to work. Don't forget to consider whether the room is to be used solely for your work – or will other members of the family be able to use it after hours?

Planning your work space
Draw a plan of your treatment room, and any other space you will use for your work. This doesn't have to be your ideal space, but must include the minimum you need to do your job comfortably, safely and efficiently.

Remember to include room for a table, chairs, equipment and any machinery, as well as for people to move around. If this is your only work space, you may need to allow room for a computer.

Armed with this plan, you will be in a strong position to evaluate any premises you visit or the suitability of using a home space. When you find the right place, you can draw a plan based on the actual room you have, knowing what you need to bear in mind. Some people opt for the ultimate freedom and run mobile businesses…

'I live in a small flat, so when I wanted to set up as an aromatherapist, I looked around at premises in town at first, but they were incredibly expensive. There was also all the cost and complication of business rates, leases, and more bills… it was a bit too much for me. In the end I became a mobile aromatherapist – I can consult with clients in their own surroundings, I don't have the expense of maintaining my own premises, and it gets me out of the flat during the day.'

Toni, mobile aromatherapist

Checklist: Planning your work space

• heating	• ventilation
• lighting	• plumbing
• flooring	• interior decoration
• equipment you need to do your job (treatment table, supplies)	• information technology (computer, printer, etc.)
• waste disposal	• reception
• storage (records, stock, equipment)	• access, including disabled access
• office furniture (desk, chair, etc.)	• telephone points
• layout	• suitable entrance
• laundry	

END POINTS

- It is important that your working space is a pleasant, welcoming place to be, as well as being suitable for the work you will be doing.
- Choices include working from home, working in a therapy centre/salon/office, or being mobile, i.e. visiting clients in their own homes.
- Many factors will affect your choice: your clients' needs, suppliers and services, communication, locality, cost, image, client base.
- Draw up a working plan of a suitable workspace before committing yourself to a particular place.

Many people choose the option of working from home, especially in the early days of setting up their business. It is a way of getting started without committing yourself to the expense of separate premises. If the business is successful, or circumstances change, it is always possible then to move into other premises.

This topic looks at the pros and cons of working from home, as well as issues to bear in mind when choosing this route.

REASONS TO WORK FROM HOME

There are many advantages to working from home. It can be particularly suitable if you:

- plan to work part-time
- have small children or other dependents
- have a large house with an obvious place to establish yourself
- don't have much money
- want to work with people in your neighbourhood
- have plenty of self-discipline.

As with most things, there are also disadvantages. It is much more difficult to close the door and forget about it.

There are also external constraints you need to know about, such as planning restrictions, insurance restrictions, the influence of the Health and Safety at Work Act and the environmental health department.

If you are planning to work from home, make sure you have the full support of your family. While it may be better for them in some ways to have you around more of the time, their lives (and possibly those of your neighbours) will also be affected.

- People will come and go – they may be clients to you, but to your family, they are strangers.
- You may be preoccupied with work and find it harder to separate work from leisure.
- Their living space may be reduced to make way for your treatment room.
- They may have to be quiet while you are working with clients.

Talk to several people who work from home. Find out why they made this decision and whether they feel it was the right one.

'I've worked from home ever since becoming self-employed. It's good to be here when the children come home from school and I can do things like put in a load of washing, and hang it out to dry in the gaps between clients. I think it helps people feel more comfortable and relaxed. We're lucky to have enough space to be able to have a room dedicated to work which can be shut away from the rest of the house.'

Counsellor, working from home

'Since I set up the salon at home, I've got to know so many of the local people – it's brilliant. People seem really pleased that they can come and have their hair and nails done, without having to trek into town, find a parking space and all that. Because I'm seeing people all the time, I don't get lonely – and I save lots of time not commuting to a salon somewhere else!'

Hairdresser, working from home

'I would really prefer to work with other people in a clinic, but I can't really justify the expense of hiring a room at the moment. My husband gets fed up with people he doesn't know coming to the house, and my mother-in-law, who lives with us, worries about security. Because I'm 'at home' all day, the rest of the family expect me to do all the usual chores, shopping, dealing with emergencies… there never seems to be any time I can call my own. When I'm better established, I'll try to find a room in a clinic.'

Massage therapist

You will find that people's responses to working from home vary enormously. How well people take to it depends a lot on their personality, their level of self-discipline and their ability to separate work from leisure.

Before you decide

Before you go too far down the route of working from home, make sure that you don't need planning permission. It is also wise to check with your mortgage lender (or landlord) that there are no restrictions on the use of the property. If you make any structural alterations to your house, you will almost certainly need to get permission from your local planning department. You may also need permission for change of use. This will depend partly on where you live and how many clients you expect to see each day. Talk to your local council to find out about planning permission, especially if you are going to use a part of your house solely for your business.

You may prefer to avoid dedicating one part of your house to business use, at least to begin with. There is nothing wrong with continuing to use your 'office' or treatment room as a sitting room. Fully lockable filing cabinets and good storage facilities should ensure that you maintain professional standards. Keep things simple until you have a well-established business and then make informed decisions about your accommodation.

Advantages and disadvantages of working from home

Here is a summary of the advantages and disadvantages for you to consider when making your decision about where to work. Everyone has different priorities, and some will be more important to you than others. You may like to compare this list with the one for working away from home in Topic 1 of this section to gain a clearer overall picture and help you think about the things that are relevant to you. Add any additional items that you think of.

> **Did you know…?**
>
> You can offset the use of part of your home against tax – including lighting, heating, water and even council tax.

Advantages and disadvantages of working from home	
Advantages:	**Disadvantages:**
• low cost	• imposes on family, and loss of family accommodation
• relaxed atmosphere for clients	• invasion of privacy
• flexible and easy to get started	• difficult to separate home from work
• draws clients from local area	• limited times of day you can offer appointments (i.e. while children are at school)
• can organise own time	• risk of theft or assault if working alone
• no travel.	• room may be inappropriate if cluttered with personal belongings
	• disruption and noise from family
	• hygiene and pets
	• relaxed, unhurried atmosphere may mean that consultations take longer
	• no reception assistance, so appointments have to be booked with gaps in between to make arrangements for paying/booking next appointment
	• isolation
	• may lead to feeling amateur.

Checklist: Working from home

Is there a suitable room which can be shut off from the rest of the house?

Is there room for your equipment, a table, treatment bed, trolleys, computer, and still space to move around?

How easy is it for people to find you?

Does your licence to practise have any restrictions over WHERE you work?

Will you (or your family) mind people they don't know coming and going?

Will you need to take additional security measures (such as installing an alarm) to protect yourself and your family?

Can you ensure that your treatment room would comply with health and safety and fire regulations (see Topics 3.1, 3.6, 3.7 and 3.8)?

Can you provide access for disabled clients?

Are there suitable toilet and hand-washing facilities?

Is there easy access through family accommodation and to toilet facilities?

Is there a suitable place for clients to wait?

Do you have a suitable place for storing records and equipment?

What will you do to 'shut off' from work?

Do you have, or are you prepared to invest in, personal indemnity insurance (see Topic 1.11)?

Do you have domestic responsibilities that would make it preferable for you to be at home most of the time (e.g. caring for young children or elderly relatives)?

Are you independent enough to enjoy working on your own?

Are you disciplined enough to benefit from the flexibility of working at home?

Would you need to obtain permission for change of use?

Are there any local by-laws that might prevent you using your home as a workplace?

Have you found out about the possibility of business rates?

Would your insurance be affected (household and professional)?

If you do decide to work from home, you will need to enlist your family's support in practical ways. They may still expect you to do everything without really realising that you too have a job. If you delegate responsibilities for certain things, you may find they respond well and are perfectly happy to help out (within reason!).

WHO DO YOU NEED TO TELL?

It is important to remember to inform everyone who might need to know that you are working from home. These people include:

- your house and contents insurers
- your mortgage lender
- city planners/local council
- your bank manager
- neighbours who might be affected.

'I hadn't realised that working from home would invalidate my existing contents insurance. My financial advisor pointed this out to me and suggested I take out a special policy which would cover the whole house, including all the equipment in my office – computers, fax machine, copier, and so on. It costs a bit more, but it's worth it in case I ever need to make a claim.'

James, psychotherapist

Car parking can be an issue if you live on a busy street or in a small village. It is unlikely to be a problem if only one or two cars are parked at any one time, but it could become more difficult if your business grows and more and more cars appear outside your house. If neighbours complain, the council may investigate and could make it more difficult for you to continue working at home.

MAKING SURE IT WILL WORK

If you decide to work at home, you will need to refine your plan of a treatment room (see Topic 1). If you drew up a sample plan, you will find it easy to draw up a firm plan, based on the room you intend to use.

Home work space
Measure up the space you have earmarked for your working area. Indicate existing fixtures (doors, windows, radiators, etc.) and then go on to work out where everything will go. Don't forget about access and disposal.

END POINTS

- Working from home can be convenient and cost-effective.
- There are some restrictions on the use of home as a workplace.
- Inform anyone who needs to know of your plans.
- Keep your family's support by sharing responsibility and making time for them.
- Consider everything carefully before making a decision.

Topic 3 Finding premises

Looking for the right place to work is, for many people, the first task in the long list of things to be done to set up a business. It can be quite a time-consuming task, as the perfect place won't necessarily turn up straight away. This topic looks at reasons why you might choose to find separate premises and how to go about doing it.

REASONS FOR CHOOSING SEPARATE PREMISES

There are many reasons why you might choose to work away from home, in separate premises.

- You may not have enough space at home.
- You may decide you want to keep home and work completely separate.
- You may be working with a partner and prefer to have 'neutral' territory.
- You may want the support of other people working in similar fields.

For these reasons and many others, many people consider that it is well worth paying for premises. Talk to people you know who have set up in business in salons, clinics or other premises. Ask them what they like and what they don't like about where they work. Find out about the disadvantages and the advantages. If you talk to people who work in your area, find out about likely rents, rates and other costs.

'I started off working from home, but was delighted when I was offered a room in our local Complementary Health Centre. There's someone there to make appointments, the centre is cleaned by a cleaner paid for out of joint funds, the security was all in place. All I have to do is turn up to see patients and then go home at the end of the day and relax.'

Reflexologist, working in a health centre

You might also be interested in the views of people who are likely to become your clients.

'I prefer going to the clinic – it seems more professional. There is always someone to answer the phone when you want to make an appointment, and a pleasant waiting room with magazines and interesting information about different therapies and treatments.'

Sandra, a client

'My hypnotherapist works from home. It sounds silly, but when I arrived I was nervous about ringing her doorbell. I was afraid that if she was with a client, the bell might wake the client up. And then if the bell wasn't answered for a while, I'd worry in case she hadn't heard it, so should I ring it again?'

Hugh, a client

WORKING AWAY FROM HOME

There are a number of different options if you are considering working away from home. Here are some of the most common, together with some of the potential advantages and disadvantages of each.

Home visiting

Advantages:	Disadvantages:
• flexible	• travel costs
• no rent to pay	• charging for travel time
• may be helpful to visit people in their own environment (giving you a better understanding of their needs)	• fewer consultations per day
	• safety issues and insurance considerations
• may be essential for some clients who are immobile.	• interruptions from other members of the client's household
	• potential to be caught up in social side of visiting, e.g. cups of tea
	• may blur professional boundaries
	• may be less easy to promote.

Renting time in an existing multi-therapy clinic or salon

Advantages:	Disadvantages:
• share overheads	• lack of control over rent increases/ closure of clinic
• only pay for the time you need	
• opportunity to build up business slowly	• contractual obligations (share cost of redecoration, etc.)
• referrals from other therapists	• limited say on decoration, fixtures and fittings
• support and professional stimulation from colleagues	
• professional environment	• any bad reputation may rub off on you
• credibility and image	• personal/professional differences with colleagues
• shared equipment	• possibility of additional therapists 'in competition' with you
• goodwill from established practice	
• reception assistance	• receptionist or environment might not be as professional as you would like.
• safety.	

Sharing leased property with other therapists

Advantages:	Disadvantages:
• shared costs	• more commitment to expenditure
• more control.	• more responsibility, i.e. employing receptionist, maintaining premises, running the business
	• falling out with partners/colleagues.

Renting space in GP surgeries or hospitals

This is a recent development which may appeal to some complementary therapists or counsellors.

Advantages:	Disadvantages:
• lends credibility to your work	• hostility from some GPs/nurses
• direct access to potential patients/ clients	• if no clearly worked out referral procedure, patients referred may be 'incurable'
• referrals from GP	• possible clashes on issues, e.g. immunization
• professional medical environment.	• pressure to be successful to gain credibility with colleagues.

Other options

Some other options for working away from home include:

• using community facilities

• buying a practice.

Checklist: Working away from home

Would you prefer to work with other people, in a centre, or simply find a space to work on your own?

How much can you afford to pay for rent, rates and any other associated charges?

Do you want the support and security of working with other people?

How far are you prepared to travel?

Have you already identified a place where you would like to work?

Would there be room for you to store equipment, records, stocks, etc.?

Would there be enough privacy for your clients?

Would you consider sharing a room with another therapist (perhaps on different days of the week)?

Do you need the routine and discipline of 'going out to work'?

LOOKING FOR PREMISES

Good sources of information for premises include:

- estate agents
- local authorities
- local library
- Training and Enterprise Councils
- your own observation – don't forget the value of walking or driving around to see what is available
- word of mouth. Tell your friends that you are looking for premises – they may know of someone with a room or work space who is thinking of letting it out, but hasn't got round to doing anything about it. Places won't always be advertised, so keep your ear to the ground.

When you begin looking for premises, the first things you will need to consider are:

- how much space you need – remember to allow storage space for equipment and supplies, a computer and desk for doing paperwork
- access to your office or treatment room – for yourself, any staff and deliveries, as well as for clients and customers
- the privacy of your client
- the image you hope to present to customers and clients, including the neighbourhood, the appearance of the building
- services and facilities – partitions or fittings, phone lines, heating, lighting, ventilation, cooking and/or refrigeration, computer networking facilities
- security – safety of your equipment; lighting arrangements; who has 24 hour access (apart from you)
- health and safety – check the provisions of the Health and Safety at Work Act

(see Section 3, Topic 1); suitable fire exits, fire extinguishers and evacuation procedure
- cost – including rent per square metre, rates, maintenance, running costs, electricity, phone bills, heating, decoration, length of lease.

'We found what seemed to be the perfect place, but there was a seven year lease, the landlord wanted three months' rent in advance, the rates were astronomical and then, to cap it all, he asked for personal guarantees. In the end, I decided it wasn't worth it, as I didn't want to risk losing my house if business didn't go well.'

If you have done a cash flow forecast (see Topic 8), set a maximum rent that you think you can afford to pay and stick to this figure! Then make lists of what is essential and what is desirable. Check what the rent includes: electricity and gas; cleaning; building maintenance; security staff; any hidden extras? Remember that the cheapest rent is not always the most economical.

Narrowing the choice

Using your plan and checklist 'Planning your work space' from Topic 1, you can evaluate the suitability of any premises, making sure that you have room for everything you need. You may also find it useful to refer to the checklists in *Healthy Business: The Natural Practitioner's Guide to Success* by N Harland and G Finn (1995). (See p. 205.)

When you visit the premises, put yourself in your clients' shoes and see what impression the premises would make on you – how easy it is to park and gain access; might some people have difficulty managing steps or narrow doorways?

'When I was looking for premises, there was one place that I fell in love with. It was part of a converted church and was wonderfully airy with columns and gothic windows. I was really tempted to overlook all the things that were wrong with it: the room was at the top of the building up a spiral staircase – hopeless for some of my clients – and parking would have been a real problem, as there was only one space allotted in the car park. In the end, sense prevailed and I decided it was no good.'

Helen, homeopath

If you find somewhere you like, draw up a quick plan, after measuring the space, just to make sure that everything will fit.

When you have finally found your premises, make sure you have a proper agreement of sale or lease drawn up by a solicitor.

END POINTS

- Think carefully about where you will work.
- If you choose an office or centre, make sure the space is suitable for your purpose.
- Make sure you can afford the rent and any related costs.
- Put yourself in your clients' shoes and imagine what it would be like for them coming to see you in any premises you are thinking of using.

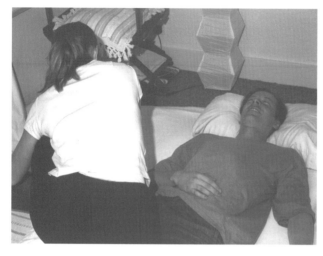

Part of establishing your business identity is deciding on the legal form your business will take. You have probably heard of terms such as 'partnership', 'sole trader' and 'limited company'. These terms have very specific meanings and implications, so it's as well to know what they mean before you start up in business.

This topic looks at what the different forms of business are and will help you decide which one is most suitable for you.

THE MAIN FORMS OF BUSINESS

The most common forms of business are:

• sole trader

• partnership

• limited company.

You may also come across the following:

• limited liability partnership

• franchise

• co-operative.

There are other forms of business, such as public limited company, but the ones above are probably the only ones relevant to you.

The form of business you decide to adopt will affect your business identity and may be influenced by the kind of work you do, your colleagues, clients and customers. It will also depend on:

• how you intend to finance the business

• the level of risk you are prepared to take

• taxation

• anyone else involved in the business

• any legal restrictions.

SOLE TRADER

This is the simplest form of business and is suitable for most people working on their own. As a sole trader, there is no legal distinction between you and your business. You are solely responsible for all decisions – and for any debts – but you are also the only person entitled to any profit you make.

Risks

As a sole trader, you are liable for all the money your business owes, in other words, your liability is *unlimited*. Your personal assets, including your house, your car, your furniture and any possessions, can be taken to pay your business debts. On the other hand, creditors can only claim against you for the bills you haven't paid. If you don't run up bills, then there is no risk.

'I don't mind having all the responsibility because I know I can rely on myself. If something goes wrong, I have only myself to blame; but when things go well, I can also take the credit!'

Jenny, beauty therapist

What you have to do

In order to set up as a sole trader, there are few formalities, but you do have to:

- register to pay Class 2 National Insurance
- inform the Inland Revenue that you are self-employed
- register with HM Customs and Excise to pay VAT if your annual turnover is more than a certain amount (see Topic 5). Your annual turnover is the amount you charge to your customers over a year.
- register with the Inland Revenue for PAYE if you employ any staff.

You may also need a licence, depending on the kind of work you are doing. Your professional body will be able to give you guidance about this.

Even if you trade as a sole trader, you can still employ other people to work for you – see Topic 12 on employing staff.

Sole traders do not have to have their accounts audited, but you may still like to employ an accountant to look after your financial affairs.

PARTNERSHIP

A partnership is an obvious choice for two (or more) people wanting to work together. Partnerships are not recognised as legal entities in England, Wales and Northern Ireland, but they are in Scotland. Like sole traders, partners do not have to submit audited accounts.

Risks

In a partnership, all the partners are liable for all the debts of the business and of any of the partners. This means that if your partner is careless with money, you would be legally responsible for paying off their business debts. The risks are therefore greater for a partnership than for a sole trader: not only do you risk losing everything, but you risk letting your partners lose it for you!

You need to have a great deal of trust in anyone you are considering working in partnership with; many partnerships fail when the partners fall out.

'A partnership is like a marriage without the romance.'

Robert Leach et al.

What you have to do

You do not have to register your business if you decide to form a partnership, but you do have to:

- inform the Inland Revenue that you are self-employed
- register to pay Class 2 National Insurance contributions
- check that any name you use for trading purposes is legally acceptable
- register for VAT if your turnover is more than a certain amount (see Topic 5)
- show your names and address on your stationery.

It is a good idea to draw up a partnership agreement, which sets out the conditions under which you agree to work together. You should do this with the help of a solicitor.

You may be able to achieve the benefits of working with someone by remaining as two (or more) sole traders, with a contractual relationship or loose association. A solicitor would be able to help you draw up a suitable contract that would protect both your interests and set out the terms of your arrangement.

'I always thought I would want to work in a partnership until I learned that I would have to pay all the debts my partner has committed us to. That put a completely different slant on things and we've decided to set up a limited company now.'

Kim, sports therapist

LIMITED COMPANY

A limited company establishes your business as a legal entity separate from you as an individual. It can be a wise choice if you are working with one or more other people; indeed, a limited company normally has to have at least two shareholders. Some people feel that a limited company lends greater credibility to their business.

Risks

You risk much less as a limited company because your liability is limited to the amount of money you have paid for shares in the business. You would not have to pay debts from your personal assets, unless you were trading fraudulently.

As a director of a new business, you may be asked for personal guarantees in order to get an overdraft, rent premises, or obtain credit from suppliers. Think very carefully before agreeing to these, as you could find yourself paying for the mistakes of others.

What you have to do

You must have two people to set up a limited company. You can start up a new company from scratch, or you may buy one 'off the peg' for between £65 and £100. You will have to:

- register a name with Companies House
- file accounts with Companies House
- send in an annual return including any changes in the directors to Companies House
- register for PAYE.

You may have to have your accounts audited at the end of each financial year, but only if you enjoy a very large turnover.

You may like to appoint an agent or a solicitor to help you set up a limited company. There are also plenty of books to help you through the process (see the Resources section of this book for suggestions).

LIMITED LIABILITY PARTNERSHIP (LLP)

A limited liability partnership is recognised as a separate legal entity. You have greater protection than an ordinary partnership because your liability is *limited*. In most other respects, the risks, benefits and requirements are the same as for a limited company.

As with a limited company, since the form of accounts for an LLP is laid down by law, it is a good idea to appoint an accountant to deal with your financial matters and to audit your accounts.

WHAT FORM OF BUSINESS SUITS YOU?

At this stage you may have a clear idea of which form of business is most suitable for you. For example, if you are going to be working on your own, then sole trader status may be the obvious thing for you. If you have other options, e.g. you are planning to work with one or more people, then you will need to consider each option carefully.

Assessing the formats

Use the following table to make a note of the advantages and disadvantages of each type of business for you, in your current situation. This will help you to decide which is the most suitable format for you to choose. If you are interested in a franchise or co-operative, you should also make a note of their respective advantages and disadvantages.

	Sole trader	Partnership	Limited company/LLP
Advantages			
Disadvantages			

END POINTS

- There are three main business forms: sole trader, partnership and limited company.
- Think carefully about the form of business you will use, bearing in mind the benefits and the risks.
- Remember that some forms have legal requirements. This is especially true of limited companies.

When you run your own business, one of your responsibilities is to make sure that the right taxes are paid at the right time. An accountant can do most of the hard work for you, but it is as well to understand the nature of the taxes you pay – you may be liable to heavy fines if you don't pay on time. Legislation and regulation change frequently, and you (or your accountant) need to be aware of current presentation requirements for tax returns.

This topic looks at types of tax and how to pay them.

> **Please note that the figures quoted in this topic are subject to change with each budget, so make sure you have current information before making any decisions based on these figures.**

TYPES OF TAX

'But in this world, nothing can be said to be certain, except death and taxes.'

Benjamin Franklin

Every country in the world imposes tax on its residents. In the UK, the main types of tax are:

- income tax, paid on income (or profit if you are self-employed)
- National Insurance
- Value Added Tax (VAT).

If you are working abroad, find out about the relevant taxes in that country.

INCOME TAX

You pay personal tax on any money you take out of the business, but the rate of tax varies depending on how much you earn.

Everyone has a personal allowance – an amount that is effectively tax-free. This varies according to your circumstances and age, but the basic amount for 2004/05 is £4,745 for a single person.

Everything you earn above the personal allowance is subject to tax. You will pay 10% on the first £2,020 you earn above your allowance. The rate then goes up to 22% for earnings between £2,020 and £31,400. You will have to pay the higher rate of 40% on any earnings over this amount.

If you are trading as a sole trader or a partnership, you will come under the Inland Revenue **Self Assessment scheme** for paying income tax and National Insurance (NI) contributions.

A limited company will be liable for corporation tax on its profits. As an employee of the company, you will pay income tax and NI contributions just like any other employee.

If you have employees (including 'casual' staff) you will need to inform the Inland Revenue. You will then receive a starter pack from the Inland Revenue, which contains everything you need to operate PAYE (Pay As You Earn) for yourself and any other employees. If you trade as a limited company, the 'employees' include yourself.

Self Assessment

The best way to deal with your tax return is to ask an accountant to prepare the figures for you. The taxation system in the UK is complicated. Accountants deal with tax and NI every day and, although you will have to pay for the service, you will almost certainly find that you save money in the long run.

However, even if you do hire an accountant, it is still your own responsibility to ensure that your tax return is submitted on time.

Keep good records

That's the bad news about tax! The good news is that you can reduce the amount of tax you pay by claiming back money you spend on expenses for the business: rent, equipment, travel, even the use of your car and your house, if you work from home. A good accountant will make sure you can claim back everything you are entitled to.

For this reason, you need to keep receipts for everything you buy for the business, as well as invoices, bank statements, statements of interest on savings accounts, evidence of any money you receive outside your business including unearned income, perhaps from rent or share dividends.

You should also be able to provide records of any other money you receive, such as maintenance following a divorce. If you are in any doubt, keep it. You can always hand everything over to your accountant to put into order.

CORPORATION TAX

If you form a limited company, you are liable to pay corporation tax if your taxable profit is above a certain amount (£10,000 in 2004). The rate you will pay varies, but the small companies rate is basically 19% on taxable profits up to £300,000 and 30% above that. Your accountant will try to reduce the amount you have to pay by claiming for all legitimate expenses.

NATIONAL INSURANCE

National Insurance is the tax paid in the UK towards providing a state pension. It also goes towards certain other benefits such as unemployment.

You will pay nothing on earnings up to £4,732 and 11% after that up to £31,720. Above that you pay 1%.

There are three different rates of National Insurance, which are reflected in the benefits you can claim.

- Class 1 applies to all employed people and is paid by both the employer and the employee. If you form a limited company, you will have to deduct NI contributions from all employees of the company and also pay an employer's contribution.

- Class 2 is paid at a flat rate by all self-employed people, whether they are sole

traders or partners. This rate is less than Class 1 but entitles you to fewer benefits.

- Class 4 is payable by self-employed people as a percentage of taxable profits.

Some accountants operate a payroll service for their clients.

'When we started up the company, our accountant suggested that they could run the payroll for us. Even though there are only two of us, it seemed like a good idea. Towards the end of every month, I phone or email the details of that month's salary for each of us. The next day, usually, an envelope arrives with all the pay details – pay slips for our records and the amount to be paid to the Inland Revenue as tax and NI. Mary even fills in the paying in slip, so all I have to do is write a cheque and send it off. All this for the princely sum of £35 per month! It would take me hours to do it and I would worry that it might not be right – I think it's a brilliant service.'

Gina, manager of a beauty salon

If you decide to do the books yourself, there are tables to help you work out how much tax and NI to deduct. It's not difficult, but you have to be careful to get it right. Get into the habit of paying the Inland Revenue every month so the amounts don't mount up. This is also important to ensure that employees are able to claim benefits they need. Remember to check on the current presentation requirements for tax returns, as the regulations change.

VAT

VAT is charged on most goods and services supplied in the UK at a rate of 17.5%. If the turnover of your business is more than a certain amount, defined in the annual budget, you must register for VAT.

For most therapists working as sole traders, VAT is not likely to be an issue, at least for the first few years. However, it is as well to understand how it works in case you become very successful very quickly!

If your turnover is less than the amount defined in the budget, you may also choose to register. This can be worth doing if you buy a lot of stock and can claim back the VAT. However, registering does have disadvantages.

- The accounting is time consuming and it's possible that, in the end, you won't save much money.
- If you are registered for VAT, you have to charge your clients the extra 17.5%; for example, if your client pays you £11.75 for a haircut, you only keep £10, but pass on the remaining £1.75 to HM Customs and Excise.

Once you have registered with HM Customs and Excise, you have to account on a quarterly basis for the tax on all the goods and services you supply (your **output tax**) and the tax on all the goods and services you purchase (your **input tax**). At the end of each three-month period, you will receive in the post a VAT return form. This must be completed by adding up all your output tax and subtracting all your input tax. The difference is the figure on which you must pay VAT. If the input tax is greater than the output tax, then you can claim money back from HM Customs and Excise.

'I've been registered for VAT for ten years and have never had an inspection. I always send in the returns on time and my accounts are completely transparent – maybe they don't think it's worth bothering. I've probably just been lucky though, as I know other people who have had two inspections during the same ten years.'

Shona, medical herbalist

'When I first registered for VAT, I used to spend all the money that came in, forgetting that a large part of it wasn't really mine to spend. Now I've got it into my head that the VAT element belongs to the government, not me. I'm just looking after it for a while!'

Roy, osteopath

Cash accounting

If your turnover is below a certain level, you may like to register for the cash accounting scheme. This enables you to account for VAT on the basis of payments received and made, rather than invoices you issue and receive. This means that you only pay VAT on money you have actually received.

END POINTS

- You have to pay income tax and National Insurance on your earnings.
- If you earn more than £58,000 per year, you must register to pay VAT.
- Your tax liabilities will probably be greater if you trade as a limited company.
- A good accountant can save you time and money and will always be up to date on current requirements for presenting tax returns.

'I've never sought success in order to get fame and money; it's the talent and the passion that count in success.'

Ingrid Bergman, Swedish actress

Unless you are very unusual, you are in business to make money – to pay the mortgage, buy food and clothes, run a car, maybe even have a well-earned holiday. You are probably also in business because you enjoy doing what you do, whatever it is.

For many people, one of the least pleasant aspects of running a business is keeping accounts. Sadly, this is also one of the most important factors for success.

You have probably heard people using terms such as cash flow, double entry, profit and loss…. When you start up your own business, you will have to become familiar with these terms and the processes they describe. The Resources section of this book has brief definitions of these and other terms, but in this topic and the next one we will look at the basics of keeping the books or 'bookkeeping'.

WHY KEEP ACCOUNTS?

Sadly, many small businesses fail because of cash flow problems. They may have plenty of work and plenty of customers,

but if there is more money going out than there is coming in, it becomes impossible to pay the day-to-day running costs. In the end, the bank will call in your chips. For this reason, people often say that cash is the lifeblood of the business.

'Annual income twenty pounds, annual expenditure nineteen and six, result happiness. Annual income twenty pounds, annual expenditure twenty pounds, ought and six, result misery.'

Mr Micawber in Charles Dickens'
'David Copperfield'

Managing your money is just one important aspect of managing the business. As your business grows, it is helpful to know how much money you are spending on, say, telephone bills or postage. If you are in control of the financial side of your business, you will be in a strong position to plan for the future; without accurate records, you will be unable to make realistic projections and estimates for your business.

You also need to be able to account to the tax inspector (and HM Customs and Excise if you are registered for VAT). You need evidence to support your declaration.

If you are a limited company (or limited liability partnership), you are required by law to submit accounts to Companies House.

WHAT RECORDS TO KEEP

At the very least, you should keep a record of your **income** (the cash coming in) and **expenditure** (cash going out). This will enable you to know, at any given moment, how much money you have.

Income

Income is the money you receive from clients, possibly from a bank loan, and perhaps from any money you or other directors or partners put into the business.

If your clients always pay immediately, it is not too difficult to keep track. If you offer credit, then you need to find a way of tracking how much people owe you and when the money is due. You can then predict how much money you will have in the future and chase people for overdue payments.

Keep any **invoices** you send out, and record when they are paid. Keep any **receipts** you give people for money you have received from them. Keep all your bank statements and reconcile them at least once a month. This will help you to keep tabs on the money going into and out of your account.

Expenses

Since almost all businesses also buy supplies and services, you will also have to keep track of the money you spend. Your suppliers will send or give you order notes and you should match these up with the receipts they will give you when you have paid for the goods or services.

Petty cash

Petty cash is the term used to refer to the small amounts of cash you use to pay for

things like stamps, stationery, and other everyday expenses. It is easy to get through a lot of money without realising it if you don't account for the cash you spend.

'Although there's only me in the business, I decided it would be best to have a petty cash box and a book of petty cash vouchers and do it 'properly'. I withdraw £50 per month as petty cash and put it in the box. Every time I take some money out, I fill in a voucher with the amount and what I've bought and put that in the box. If there's a receipt, I staple that to the voucher. At the end of the month I transfer all this information to the cash book.'

Manjindar, aromatherapist

You could note down anything you buy with petty cash in a notebook you carry with you or on a sheet of paper in the office. The main thing is to record the date, the amount and what it was for.

If you are registered for VAT, you will need to know which items include VAT so you can record this in your cash book and reclaim the VAT.

Tax deductions

One of the best reasons for keeping track of your expenses is so that they can be deducted from your income to reduce the amount of tax you have to pay. The more you can deduct, the less tax you have to pay. You can deduct almost all legitimate business expenses, including part of the use of your house, car and telephone if you are working from home.

The Inland Revenue has guidelines on how to split the cost of your phone bill and travel costs – your accountant can also help you with this. If you keep phone bills from before the business was started you can see how much they have gone up and work out a realistic division between home and business use.

It is a wise idea to save 25% of everything you earn, so that you will have enough money to pay tax. Many people like to open a second bank account for this purpose and transfer money at the end of each month. If you do this as a matter of course, you won't miss the money. If you don't follow this advice, however, you may end up with a large tax bill and no money with which to pay it.

At the lower end of the earnings scale, the Inland Revenue require only very limited information. Since the information and the form in which it is presented change so often, your accountant or the Inland Revenue will be able to tell you exactly what information you must provide.

Bank accounts

As a sole trader, you may be able to run your practice using your personal bank account. However, you must keep clear records so that you can identify every business transaction. Most personal accounts are free of regular bank charges if you remain in credit, so this may be a good way to start off your business.

The disadvantage is that your financial affairs can become rather muddled. If you do decide to open a business bank account, do shop around the various banks and building societies to find the account with the most appropriate charges and facilities to meet your needs. You should also let the bank know that you will be using the account for your business as well as personal finances, as some banks prefer you to keep things separate.

Preparing the accounts

If you keep careful records of your income and expense, it will be very easy for you or your accountant to prepare the end-of-year accounts. If you are trading as a limited company, you must submit a:

- **profit and loss account** – this is simply a statement of the income you have made and the expenditure of your business, the difference being your profit or loss
- **balance sheet** – this is a statement of the assets and liabilities of the business on a particular day, usually the last day of the accounting year. The balance sheet must give a 'true and fair state of the affairs of the business … and must comply with statute as to its form and content'.

END POINTS

You need to keep track of the money going into and out of the business so that you:

- know how much money you have in your bank account
- are able to prepare your tax return
- know how much profit you are making
- can avoid cash flow problems
- can prepare end-of-year accounts.

Topic 7 How to keep the books

Having looked at why it is important to keep records, and what records you need to keep, this topic moves on to look more closely at how to keep the books. This is quite a long topic, but it should provide a good starting point for your bookkeeping.

'A penny saved is a penny earned.'

Benjamin Franklin

SETTING UP A SYSTEM

We should point out here that keeping the books is different from keeping the accounts. Keeping the books is an important part of running your business on a daily or weekly basis. It involves, quite simply, keeping careful track of the money going into and out of your business. You are the best person to do this, although you may decide to hire a bookkeeper as your business grows.

Accounting is a more skilled job that involves analysing the books you have kept. This is best (but not necessarily) done by accountants, who are obliged to remain up to date with changes in accounting standards and to be aware of what information is required by HM Customs and Excise and the Inland Revenue. Accountants can help you make sense of the records you keep in the books.

There is no one right system for everyone. The way you record your financial trans-actions will depend on, among other things:

- the size and nature of your business
- your own financial skills and interests
- whether you want to use a computerised or paper-based system
- whether you will be relying on an accountant to do most of the work
- whether you employ staff.

The purpose of keeping records is to enable you to keep track of your **assets** and **liabilities**. This will enable you or your accountant to prepare your accounts at the end of the financial year.

'Money was invented so we could know exactly how much we owe.'

Cullen Hightower

At the very least, you will need a basic cash accounting system, so you can monitor the money going into and out of the business on a daily basis. This will not reveal the level of profit or loss you make, but it will enable you to avoid a crisis. It also makes it easy to work out your tax liability at the end of the year. The easiest way to do this is to buy a ledger for use as a cash book.

Organising the cash book

Here is a simple way of organising your cash book (or books) for payments and receipts. Remember that cash is not only notes and coins – it also refers to cheques and even credit or debit card payments.

If you are registered for VAT, you will find it helpful to have an extra column so you can record the VAT element of each transaction.

Cash receipts

Date received	Invoice number*	Customer	Amount	VAT	Paid into bank
28 04 2003	000124	John Rawlins	£20.00	£3.50	£23.50
28 04 2003	000125	P L Singh	£12.00	£2.10	£14.10

* Include the invoice number if you actually issue invoices.

Cash payments

Date paid	Cheque number	Receipt number*	Supplier/ payee	Total	Expenses	VAT
26 04 2003	––	–	Mainline Stationers	£5.17	£4.40	£0.77
28 04 2003	634576	HP3468	HP Cleaners	£44.00	£44.00	–

* Include a receipt number if you keep a file of receipts.

A simple system like this will ensure you know how much money you have coming in and going out.

You may like to analyse your expenditure further by identifying the different areas of expenditure, like this.

Date	Chq no	Payee	Total	Supplies	Telephone	Printing	Salaries	VAT
2.6.02	000201	Decleor	360.00	297.00				63.00
4.6.02	000202	BT	42.00		35.74			6.26
5.6.02	000203	Printique	110.00			90.75		19.25

If you identify the different types of expenditure and income, it will also help you identify the most cost-effective and profitable aspects of your business.

'I keep all receipts relating to the business in an envelope. At the end of the month I write everything up in a cash book, under different headings like Office supplies, Telephone, Travel, Postage, and so on. At the back of the same book I keep track of the money that comes in, based on the receipts I give clients when they pay me. I do a bank reconciliation at the end of the month, and at the end of the year I send everything to my accountant, who then draws up a profit and loss account and balance sheet and works out how much tax I have to pay.'

Nicky, homeopath

The main thing is to be methodical. Remember to include dates and names as well as amounts. It is also wise to put down how you were paid (cash or cheque).

It is much easier to write things down at the end of each day than to save them up, especially if you are seeing (and getting money from) several clients each day. It is all too easy to forget, and before you know it you have a month's worth of receipts to sort out.

Keeping regular accounts will help you

always to know where you are financially, and should help to ensure that you have enough money to pay the tax man at the end of the year.

'A bank is a place where they lend you an umbrella in fair weather and ask for it back when it begins to rain.'

Robert Frost (1874 – 1963)

Double entry bookkeeping

Double entry bookkeeping involves recording every transaction in two accounts, which helps you check the accuracy of your recording much more efficiently. It is a rather complicated system, and you do not need to know the detail.

If you are starting as a sole trader or small partnership, you will probably not need to use a double entry system. However, you should know briefly how it works since such a system may become more useful as your business grows.

Bookkeeping entries are either **debits** or **credits**. An amount that is debited to one account will be credited to another account. Each account relates to one particular aspect of the business, for example:

- cash account (for money going into and out of the business on a regular basis)
- capital account (for money put into the business by the owners)
- purchases account (for anything that is to be resold by the business, such as beauty products)
- sales revenue account (for all sales made by the business)
- accounts payable (for amounts that are due to be paid to suppliers)
- accounts receivable (for amounts that are due from customers or clients).

The debit side is at the left of the ledger page, the credit on the right, like this:

Ledger account

Debit side (Dr)   £ Credit side (Cr) £

Debits record transactions relating to purchases, expenses and any increase in the **assets** of the company (that is: cars, computers, stock, equipment, and so on).

Credits record transactions relating to income and any increase in the **liabilities** of the company.

Recording a transaction always requires a debit and a credit entry. As long as the entries have been correctly recorded, both sides of the ledger should agree when you add them up.

So, for example, when you pay a supplier's bill, you would credit the cash account because you are taking money out of that account, and record a debit in the accounts payable account, to show that you are putting money into that account. (This may seem the wrong way round. That is because you usually see the terms on bank statements, a situation where you are the customer rather than the bookkeeper. Where you yourself are the bookkeeper, the 'normal' pattern is reversed.)

You can learn more about this method of recording business transactions from books easily available from your local bookstore, or on the Internet; or you can refer to the Resources section at the end of this book.

COMPUTERISED ACCOUNTING SYSTEMS

'When I set up the centre, I thought it would be a good idea to get an accounts package for the computer. My accountant suggested Quickbooks. It's been brilliant – it takes you step by step through the whole

> **Did you know…?**
>
> The system of double entry bookkeeping was used as long ago as the 15th century by Anton Fugger who funded Christopher Columbus' first journey.
>
> Credit for its invention is usually given to an Italian, Luca Pacioli.

process of setting up your company accounts. It's very easy to use and it's helped me understand how the double entry system works. It will prepare profit and loss accounts and a balance sheet in seconds so I can always see where I am. I still send everything off to the accountant to sort out the VAT and do the end-of-year returns, but it has really helped with the everyday bookkeeping.'

Michael, owner of a holistic therapy centre

You may decide to keep your accounts on the computer. There are a number of packages designed for this purpose. Some of the most popular are:

• Quicken

• Quickbooks

• Sage

• Microsoft Money.

Computerised accounting systems work on the same principles as paper-based accounting systems. Both systems rely on regular, accurate information. If you put in the wrong figures, you will get the wrong answers; and it can be even more difficult to sort out what's gone wrong with a computer system as many functions are performed automatically.

'Garbage in, garbage out.'

Computer industry adage

However, computer packages have some advantages over paper-based systems, in that the computer will do the sums for you. It is worth asking people you know, and your accountant or bank manager, for suggestions. Then, take some time to read the manual and learn how the program works. Some programs, such as Quickbooks, have an online tutorial to guide you through the process before setting up your own accounts.

KEEPING YOUR MONEY SAFELY

Whatever the size of your business, you will need somewhere safe to keep your money. The most obvious solution to this problem is a cash register. You won't need anything too sophisticated to begin – just a simple box register which you can buy easily over the counter. At the very least, you need a lockable box with room for notes and coins.

Depending on how much money you take, you should clear the till every night or once a week, and deposit all the money in the bank. Remember to leave a 'float' – enough money to make change for clients and customers.

As your business grows, you may want to consider something more sophisticated: an electronic cash register or a networked cash register, which contains software enabling you to control stock. In both of these cases, the dealer will be involved in programming, implementing the system and training you to use it. It may be more expensive but you will get after-sales care and support.

Don't be afraid to get something simple at first, while you work out what features you actually need – you can always upgrade later. Second-hand or re-conditioned registers can also be a good – and cheaper – option.

WHO CAN HELP YOU?

Finally, don't feel you have to keep all the books yourself. We have outlined the minimum you will have to do to keep the business running smoothly and you may find that you enjoy knowing exactly how much money is going in and out of the business. On the other hand, you may prefer to use the services of a bookkeeper – perhaps on a weekly basis. If you engage an accountant, he or she will pull together all the information you provide, make sure that everything is in good order, and should also be a good source of advice on various aspects of your business.

'Remember that time is money.'

Benjamin Franklin

You can also ask your accountant to prepare your self-assessment tax return. Although this might seem like an extravagance, now that you are working for yourself, your time is valuable. A good accountant will sort out your finances quickly and efficiently, and will know ways to save you money. Meanwhile, you can carry on earning money doing what you are good at: working with your clients.

END POINTS

- There are different ways to keep track of your financial transactions.
- Find a method that works for you and then do it methodically.
- Double entry bookkeeping offers additional checks for accuracy.
- Don't forget to organise a safe place to store your money between bank deposits.
- A good accountant is not an extravagance – they can save you both time and money.

Topic 8 Budgeting and planning

Throughout this book there is an emphasis on the importance of planning, whether it relates to financial planning, recruiting staff, organising the working space or preparing a presentation. Planning is important because it helps you to work out where you want to go and figure out how to get there. In the end, this will help you to work out whether you have been successful.

In the early stages of setting up the business, financial planning is particularly important. In this topic we will look at budgeting, preparing a cash flow forecast, using spreadsheets and drawing up a business plan.

HOW MUCH WILL IT ALL COST?

Part of deciding whether your business is likely to be successful, or even feasible, involves knowing how much money you are likely to spend. This is vital if you are hoping to get a bank (or other) loan.

Start-up costs

These are one-off costs that you have to pay out initially in order to get your business up and running. If you borrow

money to finance your start-up costs, then you will have to add the interest on the repayments to the list of running costs. Start-up costs can include:

- new premises, vehicles, machines, equipment, towels
- newly designed stationery, packaging, etc.
- new stock
- initial fees connected to raising finance.

Running costs

These are the daily, weekly and monthly costs which your business has to pay out in order to survive. Running costs can include:

- telephone, Internet access, heating, lighting, etc.
- vehicle fuel and taxes
- staff salaries and other related costs
- cost of supplies
- rent and business rate community charge
- petty cash items – postage, stationery, etc.

Creating your business

Create a chart, similar to the one on the next page, listing:

- all the start-up costs your business will incur
- all of the running costs that your business has to pay out on a regular basis.

Note down any additional running costs you have to pay that are not mentioned in our list.

You may have to do some research before you can fill in the table, but it will be worth your while to give some thought to these issues now.

Start-up costs	Approximate amount
☐ Premises – deposit, premium, etc.	
☐ Moving fees	
☐ Insurance	
☐ Equipment	
☐ Stock	
☐ Stationery	

Running costs	Approximate amount
☐ Premises – rent, mortgage, etc.	
☐ Premises – business rate community charge, water, sewerage, etc.	
☐ Electricity and gas – heating, lighting, etc.	
☐ Communications – telephones, mobiles, Internet access, etc.	
☐ Staff – wages and other costs	
☐ Transport – petrol, road tax, insurances, rail fares, haulage, etc.	
☐ Marketing – advertising, packaging, brochures, web-site design, etc.	
☐ Professional fees – consultancy, accountancy, etc.	
☐ Loan repayments – including interest	
☐ Raw materials	
☐ Professional membership and professional indemnity insurance	
☐ Continuing Professional Development (CPD), e.g. journals, seminars, courses, etc.	

CASH FLOW FORECAST

In Topic 6 we pointed out that cash is the lifeblood of the business – it must keep flowing for the business to thrive. Your cash flow is likely to be closely related to your work flow; when you have busy periods, there should be plenty of cash coming in. Depending on your business, however, these may be the very times money is also going out – buying more products and supplies, paying more staff, using the phones more, etc.

Now that you have identified your start-up and running costs, you can use the chart below to note down your anticipated cash flow figures – *money coming in and going out* – for the next twelve months. This will help you work out whether your business is a viable one. It will also form the basis of any decision to lend you money.

When preparing this cash flow forecast, take into account:

- the money you expect to **receive** as a result of services or products you sell (take account of any seasonal variations you may experience in your business)
- the money you expect to **pay out** for all the things you listed above.

Using spreadsheets

A spreadsheet is a computer program specially designed to process figures. It is very useful for preparing a cash flow forecast, as you can set it up to do the calculations for you. For example, in the cash flow forecast below, you would make sure that the figure in *Total cash in hand* is the sum of *Cash in bank* and *Income from sales*. The bank balance would be that figure (£1600) minus the figure in *Total cash out* (£1200): a total of £400. Instead of having to do the addition and subtraction yourself, you can program the spreadsheet to do it for you.

Cash flow forecast for the next 12 months

	Jan	Feb	Mar	Apr	May	Jun	Jul	Aug	Sep	Oct	Nov	Dec
Cash in bank	£400											
Income from sales	£1200											
Total cash in hand	£1600											
Running costs	£1200											
Total cash out	£1200											
Bank balance	£400											

From this cash flow forecast you should be able to see:

- whether your business is going to be viable.
- any times of the year when you are likely to have a cash surplus – money in the bank
- any times of the year when you are likely to have a cash deficit – an overdraft.

'The art of prophecy is very difficult … especially with regard to the future.'

Mark Twain

If you can see that cash flow is likely to be a problem, you may be able to take preventative action; for example, cutting back on variable cost outgoings, or pre-arranging a bank overdraft to cover the cash flow deficit.

There are some other costs you have to take into consideration when planning ahead.

FIXED AND VARIABLE COSTS

You do have some control over the amount of money that flows out of the business.

Fixed costs

These costs, sometimes called overheads, are fixed and unalterable. Examples of fixed costs include:

- road tax (Vehicle Licensing Tax) -– this figure is set by the government
- loan repayments you have agreed to pay on a monthly basis for, say, a hire purchase or other fixed period loan
- rent or mortgage repayments for your business premises
- professional membership and professional indemnity insurance.

Variable costs

These costs are related to how busy you are – they increase the busier you get. They can include the cost of:

- supplies and products (such as oils, cleansers, shampoos, etc.)
- power for heating and lighting
- communications – including telephone charges, postage, etc..

Clearly, when you are working less, you will be paying less for these variable costs.

If your customers don't pay you, your cash flow will be reduced, and may mean that you are unable to pay your creditors (your landlord, the phone bill, the laundry…).

Now that you have a clearer financial picture, you should be able to prepare a business plan.

DRAWING UP A BUSINESS PLAN

A business plan pulls together and summarises all your thoughts, dreams and plans – including financial plans – for the business. It is the document you can use to persuade other people, such as bank managers, accountants, potential landlords and anyone who should know about the business, that you will be successful in your venture.

Use the following checklist to ensure that your business plan is complete.

Checklist: Contents of a business plan

The main aim of the business – often referred to as the mission statement
How you intend to achieve that aim (the product or service you are selling)
Some indication of why you think it will sell (what makes what you do special)
Where you will work
A description of the market – who your clients will be
Your estimate of prices of the services and products you offer
The approximate cost to you of the services and products you offer
An estimate of the number of sales you will make
Whether your income is likely to be more than your expenditure

This plan will also help to keep you on course in the early years of your business. An example of a business plan is included in Section 5.

FINDING SOURCES OF FINANCE

Once you have developed your business plan, you will be in a good position to approach people who may be able to help finance your business. These include:

- banks
- parents/relatives/friends
- business partners.

You may also be able to increase your mortgage in order to free up some capital to invest in your business. Beware of borrowing money against your house as, should the business be less successful than you hope, your home could be at risk. However, do make sure you have enough money to start up your business comfortably, so that you can focus on the work without having to worry too much, in the early days, about the cash flow.

EVALUATING YOUR SUCCESS

When planning for success, you need to know how you will decide whether or not you have been successful. The ability to audit the success of your business is not only an important business skill, but also a key area of your personal and professional development (see Section 2). You may find it helpful to use a checklist like the one devised by the Council for Excellence in Management and Leadership, particularly if you employ other staff, to help you evaluate how you and your business are doing and to help you improve your management and leadership skills. You can also use it in the early days of setting up your business to help you decide what is important to you in the first place. The questionnaire is available from www.managementandleadershipcouncil.org/bite/bite01.htm

END POINTS

- Planning and budgeting are key ways of deciding whether your business is going to be viable.

- Cash flow forecasts will help you see how and when the money is coming in and going out. This will help you cater for periods where you may be short of cash and may need an overdraft.

- A business plan will help you present your ideas to possible funders, and help you to keep the business on course.

- In order to evaluate success, you need to know what is important to you. A regular audit of your business and review of your business skills will also provide something against which to measure your success.

Topic 9 Communication technology

Information and communication technology (phones, faxes and computers) can be enormously good for your business, but if handled or purchased without careful thought can be a huge drain on your time, money and patience.

Choose the equipment that is right for you and your business by thinking carefully about what need it will fulfill and what you want it to do. In this topic you will look first at traditional communications technology (phones and faxes). The next topic goes on to cover computers, printers, email and websites.

Checklist: Your telecommunication needs

Do you work in one place (home, clinic, or salon)?

Do you visit clients?

Do you have someone who can take messages efficiently and professionally when you're not available?

If a call comes in when you're not available, will it be answered by a child/friend/relative?

How do customers contact you?

Is it easier if you can walk around while speaking on the phone?

Are most of your calls outgoing or incoming?

When during the day do you receive most calls?

When during the day do you make most calls?

Is personal security a concern when visiting clients?

PHONES, FAXES AND ANSWERING MACHINES

Very few complementary therapists or other small businesses could operate today without a telephone. This checklist will help you begin to think about some of the factors involved in your choice of communications technology.

TELEPHONES

A telephone is going to be an essential part of your office equipment. Think about whether you will need:

- a speaker phone
- a portable phone
- a mobile phone
- caller ID display
- memories for storing frequently used numbers.

While the price of phones has fallen, the number of features, like caller ID (which displays the number of the caller before you pick up the phone) has risen. Most modern phones have memories, so instead of writing phone numbers on a pad or Post-it notes, they can be stored in the phone's memory.

The basic choices for a corded phone are for desk or wall-mounted types, while amongst portable phones, the newer DECT phones, which have clearer reception and greater range, are replacing the older types.

ANSWERING MACHINES

As a small business, you cannot afford to miss calls from existing or potential customers, or to give the impression that you are never available. Answering machines and answering services, such as BT's 1571 service, allow your business to be responsive to the customer, even when you are not there.

'When I'm in the treatment room, the answering machine is always on so that customers can still leave messages without disturbing me. I always allow ten minutes between consultations so that I can ring people back promptly.'

Trish, herbalist

When buying answering machines, you will need to consider:

- how much space you have – combi-nation machines have the answering machine built into the phone; wall-mounted units free desk space

- the length and number of incoming messages that you are likely to receive before you have a chance to listen to the machine

- whether it is useful to be able to listen to your messages remotely, by phoning your own number and typing in a code number (essential for a mobile therapist)

- whether to use an answering service provided by your phone company.

When you set up your machine, make sure that your outgoing message is clear, short and to the point. Record it again if you're not happy with it. You should:

- make the recording when there is no background noise

- be welcoming and friendly in tone

- be brief, but speak clearly and at a measured pace

- identify your business, thank the caller for their call and explain that no one is available to take their call at the moment

- ask them to leave their name and number after the tone and say that you will get back to them as soon as possible

- let clients know when it is convenient to contact you by phone.

Many therapists advise of 'phone-in times' on a daily or weekly basis. This is particularly important if the service you offer relies on contact between patient or client and therapist. Homeopaths, for example, may have to advise on the use of remedies in an acute situation.

'I change the message on my phone every day, stating the day and date and when I will be available to talk to patients. Obviously if there is an emergency I'll ring someone back as soon as I can, but this way it is the patient's responsibility to ring.'

Sue, homeopath

If you change your message when you go on holiday think carefully about the security implications of what you say – it could be risky to announce that your salon or house will be empty for the next couple of weeks.

Finally – check your machine regularly, and respond to calls as soon as you can. Nothing will drive a client to another therapist faster than the frustration of several unanswered calls.

FAX MACHINES

A fax machine allows the image of a piece of paper to be transmitted across the phone lines to another fax machine, and printed out there. They are really useful if you want to send pictures or documents to people quickly and can't wait for the post. Fax machines can be used on the same phone line as your ordinary phone, but you can't send a fax and make a phone call at the same time.

Plain paper fax machines use ordinary A4 sheets of paper, and cost less to use (per page received) than thermal machines, which need rolls of special paper.

'The fax is great for ordering new oils and other supplies. I fill in an order form each Friday evening and fax it through to the

wholesaler as a cheap rate phone call – no need to rush down to the post box with a letter. They process it on Monday, and the stock is with me by Wednesday afternoon.'

Kate, aromatherapist

Ask yourself these questions when considering a fax machine:

- Will I ever use it?
- Do I ever need to save time by sending a fax rather than posting a letter?
- Who might want to send faxes to me?
- Do I have space for a fax machine?
- If the fax machine is in constant use, will I need another phone line?

COMBINATION AND ALL-IN-ONE MACHINES

There are telephones available with built-in answering machines, and even fax/phone/answering machine combinations. These are really useful if you want to save space, don't have many power sockets available and want a hassle-free solution to running everything on a single phone line, although you will have to pay more to get the extra features.

The all-in-one machines go even further, and can often be connected to a computer for use as a printer and scanner as well. These multipurpose machines are quite large, however, and can take up quite a lot of desk space.

'We were always running out of phone and power sockets, and the answering machine kept picking up the phone line when a fax came in, so we bought a combined fax/phone/answering machine/printer/scanner. It uses ordinary, cheap A4 paper and standard inkjet cartridges, and I can use it as a printer for letters as well. Unfortunately it doesn't make the tea!'

James, sports therapist

MOBILE PHONES

In a world where ten-year-olds carry mobile phones to school, there are shops selling them on every high street and countless adverts in the newspapers for special deals, the mobile phone would seem to be an indispensable tool for business.

'My mobile is a godsend. I travel around town most of the day, and so I can usually only check the answering machine in the evenings, or occasionally if I get home for lunch. With the mobile, clients can contact me during the day to make or change appointments. It's meant more work and fewer missed appointments – so my time is used much more profitably.'

Yasmin, travelling manicurist

However, before buying a mobile phone, and possibly committing yourself to a year's contract, you should think about:

- whether you are coping at the moment without a mobile phone
- the amount of time that your phone will be turned off and you won't be contactable anyway (such as when you're driving or in a consultation with a client)
- who you are likely to call from it, and when
- whether your clients will want to make a call to a mobile phone, which may be at a premium rate.

Security

For some mobile therapists, the mobile phone can provide a greater degree of personal security. Highly publicised

incidents, such as the Suzy Lamplugh case, where an estate agent was abducted, have convinced many people of the value of having a mobile phone.

'As I travel across quite a large rural area to give consultations, I feel less worried about the car breaking down if I have my mobile. It also gives me a better sense of personal security, and if I'm meeting a new client, I arrange to call a colleague after the consultation.'

Sian, Feng Shui consultant

Appropriate and inappropriate uses

Receiving calls on a mobile phone may be appropriate for making appointments (as long as you have your diary with you) but completely inappropriate for discussing more personal issues, such as a reaction to a recent treatment. Make arrangements to speak to your client at a more appropriate time and place. Remember that, if you are providing complementary medical treatment, your case notes are medico-legal records. It is essential to keep clear records of all communication with patients – this could be difficult if you are talking on a mobile phone while on the move!

Costs

When choosing a mobile phone, the call plan (which defines your monthly payment and call rates) is probably the most important factor; then the coverage that the network offers in your area, particularly if you live and work further from the large urban areas; followed by battery life and phone size. The least important issue is the number of added features that the phone provides beyond the basic functions – you will probably never use most of them.

Calculating costs

Pick up a booklet from a mobile phone retailer outlining the call plans that different phone providers offer. Work out when you think you will make most of your calls, and how long they will be.

Calculate your monthly bill on various plans and compare them before choosing or changing. If you find the maths tricky, several companies have calculators on their websites, such as http://www.buy.co.uk/ but remember that these are still sales tools!

There are other possible costs that a mobile phone may incur for you and your business.

- It may be stolen or damaged and have to be replaced.

- Unauthorised calls may be made on a stolen phone.

- Changing tariffs or providers may cause problems if you decide not to take your existing mobile number with you.

'I changed my mobile for a newer model with a different deal and saved £5 per month. What I'd overlooked was that it would cost me £127.45 to have my business cards reprinted with the new number on them, and I've also lost some customers who couldn't get hold of me when the old number went out of service.'

George, mobile physiotherapist

END POINTS

- Think carefully about what you need before committing yourself to a particular model of phone or fax.

- Think about the phone calls you make and receive – how many, how long and when.

- Think about how many calls you miss.

- Consider the space available and the number of power and phone sockets.

- Compare mobile phone charging plans and upgrade costs before deciding which one to opt for.

Topic 10 Information technology

Choosing the correct computer equipment is an extremely important decision for your business. Making the wrong choice – and saddling yourself with an unsuitable computer system – can cost you a huge amount in terms of time and money lost. The effect on your business could be disastrous. This topic looks at the factors you should consider when choosing a computer system.

DO YOU NEED A COMPUTER?

This is the most important question. If you don't need it, don't buy it. A computer system can be a major investment and you should be making your decisions in the light of cold commercial reality. Beware the salesperson who insists that you need an entire (and undoubtedly expensive) office automation package, with a scanner, printer, fax-modem, email and expensive PC.

A computer should only be bought for one of two reasons:

- it will solve a problem or meet a need you have clearly identified. For example, creating mail shots to potential clients; storing and managing customer appointments and details; stock control

- a computer system will help expand your business into areas that you could otherwise not handle.

'I thought that we should have a computer – I didn't think about why. A very persuasive salesman in the local business computer centre sold me a complete system that cost over £3,000 – but I just can't get the hang of the thing, and the supplier has not been at all helpful. It was quicker to go back to doing things by hand. At the moment my son uses it to play Tomb Raider.'

Toni, salon owner

> **Did you know...?**
>
> The government provides special ICT tax allowances for small businesses.

Checklist: Factors in choosing a computer system

Have you used a computer before?

Do you know how a computer might help your business?

How much can you afford to pay?

Can you maintain the computer or will you have to pay someone to do it?

Are there any reputable suppliers near you?

Is there space for a computer?

Where would you get training on using the computer?

Unlike a TV, the process of buying a computer system doesn't stop when you leave the shop with the machine. In order to do something useful, a computer requires appropriate **software** to run on it. Someone in your business needs to be able to use that software. To generate any printed output you will need a printer. The computer and the printer will both need regular feeding with consumables (disks, paper and printer cartridges) and so, like a puppy, a computer is a commitment and not just for Christmas!

WHAT WILL YOU USE THE COMPUTER FOR?

Before you buy a computer, you must decide what you want to do with it. Think about whether you want to:

- calculate costings and estimates
- keep track of clients' appointments and details
- write letters and create faxes
- generate mailshots to clients
- send and receive email
- keep your accounts.

CHOOSING SOFTWARE

Without the right software, the computer is useless to you. Once you have decided what you want to do with the computer, you can identify the software packages needed to do those things.

- To calculate costings and estimates, you can use a type of software package called a *spreadsheet*.
- To keep track of customer appointments and details, you might use a *database*.
- To write letters, you would use a *word processor*.
- To generate a mail shot to clients, you would use the database and word processor in combination.
- To send and receive email, you will need an *email* package
- To keep your accounts, you would need an *accounts* package.

Here are the names of some typical software packages and what they do.

Maker	Software title	Use
Microsoft	Word	Word processing
Microsoft	Access	Database
Microsoft	Excel	Spreadsheet
Intuit	Quickbooks	Accounting
Microsoft	Outlook Express	Email

You will have noticed that four out of the five software packages listed above are made by Microsoft. This is because they are the most successful (and biggest) supplier of PC software in the world. The Microsoft products listed above are also available together as Microsoft Office or Office Professional, so you can buy software that is capable of meeting most of your office needs in one pack. When you have worked out what software you will need, find out how much it will cost.

Your professional body may also have information about specialist software.

CHOOSING THE COMPUTER

Now you can think about the computer that you need to run the software. PCs and Apple Macintoshes both have friendly user interfaces that you control using a keyboard and a mouse. What matters to you is that the computer will run the software that you need. You should think about whether:

- friends or colleagues can lend advice and support on one type or the other
- there are dealers supplying either type of computer conveniently close to you
- there are suppliers, recommended by colleagues or friends, close by.

You also need to consider how much memory you will need to run the programs you will be using.

Unless you really know what you are doing, don't buy a second-hand computer. New computers:

- cost only slightly more than second-hand ones
- have a warranty
- are likely to be more up to date
- are often 'bundled' with some basic software, such as word processing and possibly money management packages.

PRINTERS

If you want to print out letters, invoices, leaflets, etc., that you have created on your computer, then you need a **printer**. Printers come in two types – **laser** or **inkjet**.

Affordable laser printers are usually black and white. Inkjets are available as colour printers at low prices. The quality of printed text from a laser printer will be better than that from an inkjet printer, and it will also print out pages faster. If you want to print out lots of letters or quality mail shots, then a laser printer is probably a better bet.

If you will need to print colour materials, and are not so concerned about the sharpness of the print or the slower print speed, then an inkjet may be for you.

Running costs differ also – inkjets tend to cost more per page in terms of ink cartridges than lasers do. This is especially the case for colour printing, as the cost of colour cartridges is high, and colour prints often have a lot of colour on the page.

'My laser printer is brilliant. I can just update my sandwich list and then print off fifty copies for distribution to the businesses on my round every week – they are much more professional than my old hand-written ones, and it's cheaper (and more flexible) than getting them printed.'
Dave, sandwich van operator

You may find, if your printing needs are simple, you don't have much space, and you need a fax, that an all-in-one machine is ideal for you. See Topic 9 on communications equipment for more details.

TRAINING

As we discussed earlier in this topic, it's not much use having a computer, software, printer, etc., if you can't or don't use it. This is where you need training. There are many good and affordable sources of training available to small business users. Look at the evening or day courses offered by your local FE colleges and secondary schools – these are usually very good and much more affordable than those offered by dedicated computer training organisations. They are also local, and usually run in the evenings, so they don't interfere with your work. You could even go before you buy a computer, to make sure you will get along with it. Look for training courses on the software packages that you identified as being useful to your business.

If you want to get a better and more general grounding in general computer use, look at courses such as the European Computer Driving Licence (ECDL) that is offered by many local colleges.

ONCE YOU'VE GOT THE COMPUTER

Set the computer up according to the guidance on position and screen placement given in the manual. Be careful of reflections from windows, and look out for trailing flexes. Buy a proper computer desk and chair and adjust them correctly. Think about security – computers are popular targets for thieves. Don't forget to register with the Office of the Data Protection Registrar if you intend to keep an electronic database of clients' personal details.

END POINTS

Ask yourself these key questions before buying computer equipment.

- What business needs will the computer fulfil?
- What software will meet those needs?
- What machine is needed to run the software?
- What training do I need to operate the software?
- How much time will it take to maintain the system?
- How much will the consumables cost?
- Where will I put the computer?

Topic 11 Legal issues (including insurance)

If you are starting up in business, there are some things you must do to ensure that you are within the law. The laws that are most likely to affect you are covered in more detail in Section 3 of this book, but we will give an overview here of some of the more general aspects of the law affecting small businesses. Bear in mind that legislation is constantly changing and you need to keep up to date. One good reason for joining a professional body is that they will alert you to changes in legislation and regulation, and can advise you about the effects of legislation on different aspects of your work.

In this topic we will examine some of the legal requirements for setting up a business and, in particular, the need for insurance.

'The best armour is to keep out of range.'

Italian Proverb

LEGAL REQUIREMENTS FOR SETTING UP IN BUSINESS

The legal implications are slightly different depending on the form of business you choose.

'We had been in business for nearly a year when our accountant phoned up one day to ask us whether we had any business insurance. Since our computers and equipment were covered on another policy, I didn't know what he meant until he explained about public liability and business interruptions insurance.
Our office is in our house, so he put us in touch with a specialist broker who set us up with one policy which covers public liability (in case anyone trips over the doorstop), employer's liability (in case one of our employees sues us), all our computers and equipment and, best of all, business interruption. That means, if there is a fire or any of our equipment is

damaged, the insurance company will make a payment to cover the lost earnings.'

Ria, counsellor and writer

INSURANCE

Insurance is one of those necessary evils. Although you may resent paying for it, if you don't have it when you need it, your problems will be much worse. When things do go wrong, insurance is worth every penny of every premium.

'Prevention is better than cure.'

Proverb

There are some forms of insurance that you are required by law to have – and others that are simply advisable. Your priorities will be partly dictated by your business and the potential threats. If you run a sports clinic for underprivileged youngsters in a poor area, you are likely to have expensive equipment without which you could not do your work. The building and contents may be at risk from theft, fire or vandalism, so you will need a good policy to cover the building and its contents.

If, on the other hand, you are a counsellor working from home, you won't have any expensive equipment, and theft is less likely because you will probably be around

> **Did you know...?**
>
> Even if you work from home, you are required by law to have public liability insurance.

59

Checklist: Initial legal requirements		
Decide which items in this column apply to you and then tick the right column when you are sure you have taken the necessary steps.	**This applies to me**	**I have complied with this**
Gain permission from the local authority or council for change of use of existing premises (e.g. using a bedroom in your house as a hairdressing salon) (see Topic 2 of this section)		
Register with Companies House (see Topic 4 of this section)		
Submit audited accounts (see Topics 4 and 5 of this section)		
Planning permission for any structural changes to the building in which you will work (e.g. adding an extension to your house to use as a treatment room) (see Topic 2 of this section)		
Register for VAT if turnover is over the limit (£58,000 in 2004) (see Topic 5 in this section)		
Insurance (public liability, professional negligence, buildings, fire, theft, change from household policy, etc.) (see below)		
Local by-laws may require a licence to practise or operate (necessary for some therapists – check with your professional body and local council) (see Section 3 Topic 1)		
Pay National Insurance and Income Tax for staff (see Topic 5 in this section)		
Keep records of accounts (see Topics 4, 5, 6 and 7 of this section)		
Have a proper agreement of sale or lease drawn up by a solicitor (see Topic 3 of this section)		
Draw up contracts of employment (see Section 3 Topic 2)		
Know about and comply with Race, Sex and Disability Discrimination legislation (see Section 3 Topic 3)		

much of the time. But you will need professional indemnity insurance to protect you against any claims made against you by a dissatisfied client.

The two most important forms of insurance you need are:

- public and employer's liability insurance
- professional indemnity insurance.

PUBLIC AND EMPLOYER'S LIABILITY INSURANCE

If you have no other insurance, you *must* have public and employer's liability insurance. This will protect you if a client or member of your team trips over the front door step or takes a tumble down the stairs and decides to sue you. It is a bit like the third party element of the insurance on your car – this insurance is to protect other people as well as you.

PROFESSIONAL INDEMNITY INSURANCE

Occasionally, even the most careful and experienced professionals make mistakes and accidents happen. A client who is unhappy with a treatment may decide to sue. Sadly, the enthusiasm for litigation when something goes wrong is becoming increasingly common in the UK.

Clients can only claim successfully if you have been unprofessional, negligent or if there has been an accident. However, proof that you have been acting professionally includes:

- keeping records of the treatment and any problems associated with it
- having a procedure in place that explains any risks, after effects or likely consequences of any treatment to the client both generally and to that client in particular and

- getting clients to sign forms that they understand and that they are satisfied with the treatment
- dealing with complaints from clients and any signs of discomfort/ unhappiness immediately.

Clients cannot successfully claim against you for unprofessional behaviour/ treatment if they are simply unhappy with the treatment. If a client is unhappy you need to resolve this by using customer care skills. (Section 2 covers communicating and dealing with clients and complaints.) Don't wait for the unhappiness to fester into a claim.

The legal costs of defending a claim, even if it has little chance of succeeding, can be high – much higher than your premium.

Public liability and professional indemnity insurance are likely to be available through the professional body associated with your particular field of work. In order to qualify for this insurance, you will almost certainly have to join the organisation and agree to practise according to its professional code of practice. ITEC has such a policy for its members. See Section 5.

It is important to realize that insurance is not a 'cushion' that you can use to sort out claims from clients. If a successful claim is made against you, your insurance in the future may be more costly or even not available. So it is far better to prevent claims happening in the first place.

Product liability insurance

If you use any products, oils, creams, waxes, etc., on your clients, you will need to be insured against damage that might be caused by the products. If you sell those products to your clients, you will need to ensure the policy covers sales.

Products used for particular treatments should only be sold to clients whom you have seen personally and whose medical/health condition you understand.

Buildings insurance

If you own the premises in which you work, they must be insured. If you work from home, the fabric of the building will be covered on your house insurance policy, but check to make sure that working from home does not invalidate the policy.

If you lease the premises, check with your landlord. Nine times out of ten, insurance will be bought by the landlord and the cost passed on within your rent.

If you lease a room or a chair or treatment table in a salon or clinic, find out whose responsibility it is to arrange insurance cover – and make sure you are covered!

Either way, any insurance for the building must be adequate to cover the cost of rebuilding it to an equivalent standard, and remember, the cost of rebuilding does climb. A regular check on the value of the building is always a good idea.

Having protected yourself against crippling lawsuits and the expense of having to repair or rebuild the place in which you work, you can begin to think about other kinds of insurance.

Permanent health insurance

If you are self-employed, this can be a great help if you become ill. This kind of policy will pay a percentage of your normal income if you become ill and unable to work. Make sure that the cover is relevant and, as with all insurance policies, take time to read the small print and the exclusion clauses.

'When I started working for myself, one of the first things I did was take out permanent health insurance so that there would be money to pay the mortgage and feed the children if I were to become ill. It paid off after a few years when I had shingles and couldn't work for a month – it was brilliant to have a bit of money coming in and it tided us over a difficult time.'

Naomi, holistic health consultant

Office contents insurance

It is advisable to have insurance to cover your business for all equipment within the building and provide some protection if you are travelling with, say, aromatherapy oils, exercise machines, laptop computers, etc.

Make sure there is adequate protection – 'new for old' could be a good idea for computer equipment. Computers tend to devalue quickly, but you would probably want to spend about the same again as the original outlay to ensure you have bought the latest technology. Remember to keep receipts for any equipment you purchase.

Be generous with your limits – a few old desks and filing cabinets may not appear to be worth much, but if you had to replace them in a hurry, the cost would be hard for many businesses to handle.

Business interruption insurance

This kind of insurance could make the difference between survival and collapse. If your place of work is affected by a fire or flood, for example, you will have no place to work. Many home workers policies and standard packages come with business interruption as standard. A good policy will cover the cost of a temporary workplace (including renting or leasing somewhere) and a move to the new premises, including the cost of diverting your telephone calls and setting up new telephone lines.

Check the small print to make sure that the policy offers cover applicable to your needs and adequate in terms of financial recompense. Be warned, business interruption will only come into effect if the peril was insured. For example, if there is a power surge that results in all the telephone lines going dead and the computer hard discs being erased, your claim will only be successful if the policy covered power surges.

Car insurance

If you intend to use your car for work, check your policy very carefully to make sure that you will still be covered. If you are a mobile therapist, make certain that your equipment is covered, either on your car insurance or on your contents insurance.

END POINTS

- When you set up in business, you need to be aware of certain legal requirements.

- You must have insurance to cover professional, public and employer's liabilities.

- It is wise to insure against certain other eventualities – you will have to decide which are most important to you and your business.

- When taking out insurance, *always read the small print* to make sure the policy covers what you want it to cover.

Topic 12 Finding and keeping staff

If you are successful, or planning to be successful, you may decide that you want someone (or several people) to share the load. You will need to recruit some staff.

As well as paying attention to employment legislation (covered in Topic 2 of Section 3), you need to make sure you find the right people for the job. Then, once you have found them, you will want to hold on to them…. This topic looks at the issues that arise once you decide to employ people.

WHY EMPLOY MORE PEOPLE?

There are plenty of advantages to having more people around to do the work. You will be able to take on more clients and offer more treatments; you may be able to spend more time with each client, providing a more personal service.

'I had been running my own massage clinic for 12 years when I finally came to the conclusion that I didn't need to work quite this hard. So I took the plunge and decided to take on a couple of assistants who would be able to do the more straightforward treatments for me. I was lucky enough to get two people who had recently qualified and who are excellent.

They've given me some new ideas and ways of working too, and the clients seem happy enough.'

Lisa, massage therapist

The downside of employing more people is that you will need more space (unless you have plenty of room already), you may need to invest more capital (to buy more equipment, chairs, etc.) and your overheads will rise.

There may come a time, though, when you simply cannot do all the work yourself, and the choice to take on someone else becomes inevitable.

FINDING THE RIGHT PERSON FOR THE JOB

Successfully employing staff means finding the right person for the job. This sounds easier than it is, but careful thought at the beginning of the process will reward you later.

If you employ the wrong person, you may be stuck with them for a very long time, given the difficulties of dismissing staff. So, how can you make sure that the person you employ has your own high standards and the appropriate skills for the job?

Begin by giving careful thought to what the job is, then think about the kind of person best suited to doing the job. If you need someone to carry out reflexology treatments or Reiki, you need someone with the appropriate qualifications and experience.

On the other hand, if you need someone to answer the phones, pick up the towels, sweep the floor and tidy up, you do not need someone with specialist qualifications – such a person would be bored and then would not do a good job.

Answering the following questions will help you to write a formal **job description** and a **person specification**.

Job descriptions

A job description will help you to clarify what is needed, and every employee should have one. This document forms the basis of your contract with the employee. Employees only have to do what is in their job description – you can ask them to do more, but you can't make them.

Many job descriptions are too vague, listing only duties rather than what the employee is expected to achieve. A good job description includes **goals** and **targets** for the employee, so that they know what they are trying to achieve and you know how to measure their performance.

This will give you a good basis for writing a job description for any staff you hope to recruit. There is a sample job description in Section 5.

So, now that you know what the job is, what kind of person do you need to do it?

Person specifications

The person specification sets out your expectations of the person in terms of:

- qualifications
- skills
- knowledge
- personal qualities.

Good advertisements often include at least an element of a person specification:

> ### Come and join our busy salon!
> You will need NVQ Level 3 in Hairdressing, two years' experience of cutting hair, excellent communication skills, patience and a good sense of humour!

There are sample job advertisements and person specifications in Section 5. Working with people can be enjoyable, rewarding and fun, but it can also be tiring and stressful. Not only do you and any staff have to be able to get along with clients, but you also need to be able to work together as a team, however small. It is unfair on the new employee, as well as yourself and any existing staff, to employ someone who is just not going to fit in.

DISCRIMINATION

If you are employing other people, you also have to take into account the laws governing sex, race, age and disability discrimination. Section 3 deals with this topic in more detail, but the key point is that your job has to be open to *anyone* who meets the person specification.

If you want your business to be a lively, interesting, growing place, then you need a variety of people working there, who can talk to all kinds of clients and bring different points of view to work.

'When we advertised for a sports massage therapist, I realise now that in my mind's eye I intended to employ a young man. When the best candidate by far turned out to be an older woman, I had to stop and re-examine my own ideas. I was worried that she wouldn't get on with the clients, many of whom are young blokes, but she seems to be doing just fine. Because she's a bit older (and, as it happens, has sons of her own), she talks to them easily. She's also good with the other staff – very calm and supportive. Now I just want to hang on to her!'

Darrell, manager of a health club

PREPARING FOR INTERVIEWS

Once you have some people who may be interested in working with you, you will want to meet them, so that you can find out more about each other. Before inviting anyone for an interview, it is a good idea to check their qualifications and references so that you don't waste your time or theirs.

The best interviews are a result of good preparation by everyone involved – and a bit of luck. You may have experienced, perhaps from the other side, the interview where you and the other person just seem to hit it off immediately. This may be a good indication that the person is right for the job, but beware of being seduced by the kind of person who has highly accomplished social skills but perhaps little else to offer! Make sure you are satisfied that the person can do the job and then, by all means, chat about their hobbies or the interests you have in common.

What to ask

You should have at least a mental list of questions you want to ask. Try to vary your questions between open questions (those requiring some explanation as an answer) and closed questions (which require only a 'yes' or 'no' answer). Be careful not to discriminate against an applicant through the questions you ask. Remember to listen to the answers, and do make some notes – you will be amazed at how quickly you will forget details after the interview.

Here are some questions to help you get started.

- What attracted you to this job?

- What do you consider your strengths and weaknesses to be?

- What do you like best (and least) about your current job (or college course)?

- What would you like to be doing in two (five) years' time?

- How would you handle a situation like X?

- What do you do in your spare time?

You will find more guidance on different kinds of questions and general communication skills in Section 2.

If you are not quite sure about someone, you may want to observe them doing a demonstration treatment. It would be courteous to give the person some warning so they can prepare adequately. You may want the demonstration to be carried out on another member of staff, or you may offer reduced rates to people who are prepared to have treatments carried out by trainees or new staff.

Some people are very nervous at interviews and fail to do themselves justice. Try to be sympathetic if you are aware of this, and have a few less challenging questions which will help to put the person at ease. Remember how you felt when you have been interviewed in the past – what made it easy for you to talk, and what made it more difficult? Good interviewers are genuinely interested in people and in how they may be able to contribute to the business.

The good employer provides:	The good employee provides:
• wages or salary and other benefits (including sick pay and holiday entitlement)	• time – a certain number of hours each day; skills and knowledge
• a pleasant and safe working environment	• punctuality and reliability
• freedom from discrimination	• loyalty to the employer
• opportunities to grow and develop in the job, including encouragement and feedback on performance	• willingness and commitment to develop and improve
• trust in employees' ability to do the job	• confidentiality about all matters relating to the business
• clear expectations of the job	• willingness to perform the relevant tasks to the requisite standard
• respect and honest communication.	• respect and honest communication.

KEEPING STAFF

Once you have found the right person for the job, you hope they will stay and become a permanent member of the team. This will generally happen if you are happy with the work being done, and the employee is happy with the terms and conditions of employment.

The notion of a contract is a two-way arrangement.

If you and your employees can reach an agreement like the one outlined above, you are likely to be able to work contentedly together for some time.

DISCIPLINE AND GRIEVANCE

If there is a problem with a member of staff, the best thing you can do is to deal with it as soon as possible; don't ignore it and hope it will go away. Talk to the person and try to find out what is bothering them – they may have personal problems that are affecting their work. Acknowledging any difficulty of this nature, and encouraging the person to seek appropriate help, may resolve the problem as far as you are concerned.

If the problem persists or is more serious, you will need to follow a formal disciplinary procedure. This procedure should be set out in the contract of employment (see the sample contract in Section 5). Generally, employers should give a verbal warning, followed by a written warning, and then a final warning before actually dismissing someone.

There are a few situations which are so serious that you may dismiss the person on the spot. These are:

- gross misconduct or breach of contract (e.g. theft, drunkenness, drug abuse, violence)
- criminal offence.

Occasionally, members of staff may have a grievance about you or the salon or clinic.

There should also be an established grievance procedure which is likely to involve putting the grievance in writing, with the expectation of an interview to try to resolve the difficulty.

If you are a sole trader or small partnership, these issues are unlikely to concern you. However, if you grow and expand, it is possible that you may encounter difficulties one day and it is best to know how to deal with them.

END POINTS

- There are advantages and disadvantages to taking on staff.
- You have legal obligations when employing staff, especially with regard to equal opportunities, and health and safety.
- Clear expectations of the job and the person are set out in the job description and person specification.
- Once you have recruited the right staff for the job, make an effort to keep them.

Topic 13 Keeping and storing records

Keeping careful records of your clients is an important part of running a professional practice. It is good for a hairdresser to know what colour dyes are used on your hair. It is essential for a therapist to have more complete records about their clients' general health. In this topic, we will look at setting up and keeping client records.

WHY ARE CLIENT RECORDS IMPORTANT?

When you meet a client for the first time, one of your tasks is to gain a clear picture of their needs. This will help to ensure that you meet the client's expectations, whether you are carrying out a particular therapeutic treatment, doing someone's hair or polishing their fingernails. This is simply good sense so that you can, ultimately, give your clients what they want, but also so that you will have a record if anything goes wrong.

In Section 2, we look at the initial consultation and at listening skills – you

should look at both these topics in conjunction with this one.

'I was really impressed to discover that my hairdresser has a record card for me – it has obvious things like my name, telephone number and address, and it includes the colours he's used on my hair. It's reassuring to know that, even if he was ill, someone else could do my hair using the same colours!'

Sophie, client

Checklist: How client records can help you.

Tick the ways that apply to you.

☐	You know how to contact clients if, for any reason, you have to cancel an appointment or need to talk to them about something.
☐	Filling in the client record card is a good way to get to know the client.
☐	You need to know what has brought the client to you – the problem or issue they face – so that you can make an appropriate plan.
☐	As you work with clients, you need to know what works and what doesn't work, so you can do more of the right thing and less of the wrong thing.
☐	If there is a health emergency, you need to know who to contact – a close relative or a doctor.
☐	If you are ill and someone else has to take over your clients, up-to-date records will help them to do the right thing.
☐	A record card can serve as a useful aide memoire, especially if you see a lot of clients.

In order to protect yourself against possible claims, whenever you provide health or beauty treatment to clients, you should maintain and keep client record cards according to the advice of your professional body. Every treatment should be recorded, and it is wise to ask the client to sign a statement of satisfaction after the treatment.

For some treatments, you should test the client or patient for adverse reactions (this is often done as a patch test). You should refuse to treat the client until he or she has had the test. Even if in certain circumstances (such as in a hotel salon or clinic), the client would be willing to sign a waiver which makes it clear that he or she has agreed to the treatment without the test, this still leaves you liable to a claim against you as, professionally, you ought to have done the test.

PREPARING A CONSULTATION RECORD

Many places keep client records on computer, but you may prefer to have an old-fashioned card for each client. You need to be aware of the implications of the Data Protection Act (covered in Section 3) and you will need to register if you do keep any personal information on computer. However you choose to keep records, the important thing is to ensure that you obtain the necessary information.

You can use the following pro-forma to help you design a card or a computer form. The exact details you need will depend on your particular area of work – if you are cutting hair you probably don't need a medical history, for example. Remember to leave enough space for the information you need. There is no point having a record card with so little space that you can't read your own writing! You can add new cards or pages for later sessions.

Client record card	
Client's name	(include a note of what he or she likes to be called)
Address	
Daytime telephone	
Evening telephone	
GP name and phone	
Brief medical history	
Any contraindications to treatment	(e.g. allergies, existing medication)
Client's lifestyle	(e.g. stressful job, lots of sport, six children)
Client profile	(include here any strong religious, moral or social beliefs that your treatments might need to take into consideration)
Treatment plan	(bear in mind anything which might affect the treatment, such as work schedule, particular beliefs, existing conditions, etc.)
Client's consent to treatment	(you may like to get the client's signature, but at the very least, make sure the client understands the nature of the treatment and any implications)

If you agree on a course of treatments, you might make a note of any fees you agree or any particular methods of payment. You may also need to indicate how many treatments the person has had e.g. using tick boxes, or writing down the dates when you see the person.

You will need most of this information from a client the first time you meet. Topic 15 in Section 2 covers other aspects of the first contact with clients.

'I find that filling out the client record card is a really helpful way of handling the first session, especially if the client is a bit shy. It gives a good structure to our conversation without seeming as though you're probing. I think it feels very professional to most clients – they are happy to give you all kinds of personal information if it's for your records.'

Debbie, beauty therapist

KEEPING THE RECORDS UP TO DATE

As time goes by, you need to keep the records up to date. It is important to note:

- the dates when you see clients and what is done
- any home care advice (and whether the advice has been followed)
- the effects of any treatments (good or bad)
- how the client is feeling, including any changes in lifestyle
- any agreed changes to the plan
- whether (and how much) the client has paid.

Adding brief notes at each session will ensure that you continue to work *with* clients and, hopefully, meet their expectations. A follow-up page might look like this:

Date seen	
Patient consent to treatment	(signature)
Summary of the session	(include here any progress since last time, any particular problems and what was done this time)
Any changes to your plan?	
Home care advice	(e.g. not drinking coffee, doing a particular exercise, using a particular product, etc.)
Payment received	
Emergency contact	

If you provide health treatments, you are obliged to maintain good clinical records. Your professional body should have a code of conduct that will lay down good practice guidelines on issues such as clients' access to their records, and communication with other practitioners involved with the patient's case.

'After each session with a client, I spend five minutes writing down briefly what progress has been made, what we worked on in the session and what the client wanted to sort out. Although I have quite a good memory, it's really helpful to be able to look back, just before a session, to remind myself what we should be doing.'

Daniel, shiatsu masseur

END POINTS

- Keeping careful records of your clients is an important part of running a professional practice.

- If you keep records on computer, you need to comply with the Data Protection Act.

- Keep records up to date and avoid building up a backlog of record-keeping.

- Professional bodies often have designed forms suitable for the therapies and treatments related to their profession. ITEC Professionals provides such materials.

Section 2

Relationships, professionalism and ethics

Topic 1 Being professional: preparing yourself and your surroundings

This topic looks at what it means to be a professional – the preparations you need to make to reassure your clients that you work in a professional way. This means presenting yourself well and making sure your surroundings (your reception area and practice room) are appropriate and comfortable.

Topic 2 looks at other aspects of professionalism: time-keeping and working within the limits of your expertise.

WHAT IT MEANS TO BE PROFESSIONAL

When clients consult you, they are placing their confidence in you as a professional. They are entrusting their health and/or well-being to your care. Professionalism is about earning and keeping the trust of your clients. It is also about taking pride in yourself and your skills as a therapist.

Professionalism

Think about the last time you had really good service from someone such as a car mechanic, a hairdresser or your dentist.

- What was good about what they did for you?

- In your view, what made their service to you really professional?

'The mechanic didn't make me feel like a fool – he took me seriously and kept asking me questions until he found what was causing the knocking in the engine.'

Isabella

'I love going to my hairdresser. The atmosphere is always warm and friendly. They offer you a cup of coffee, and there are always fresh flowers on the reception desk.'

Lily

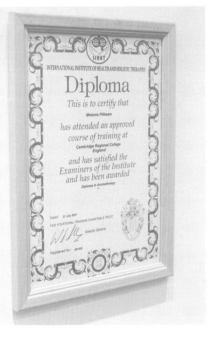

'Our dentist is great with children. There is always someone there to help with the pushchair, and a really nice play area for the children. It makes you feel that they care about you and want to make things as easy and pleasant as possible. I call that "professional".'

Sheila

HOW YOU PRESENT YOURSELF

What should I wear?

In many professions it is customary to wear an overall or uniform over your street clothes. Decide how many professional outfits you will need; as a minimum, have 'one to wash and one to wear', but you may need an extra change of clothes if the set you are wearing becomes dirty.

In some kinds of work, you can choose your own clothes. What you choose depends on the sort of work involved, but as a basic rule they should be clean, comfortable and neat. For example, for a sports therapist, appropriate clothing might be a polo shirt and either tracksuit bottoms

Checklist: Preparing yourself to meet clients

	Yes	No
Have I removed all my jewellery (except a wedding band and stud earrings)?		
Do I smell OK? Clean and free from body odour?		
Does my breath smell fresh?		
Have I remembered not to use perfume?		
Is my hair neat, clean and tied back (off my collar and away from my face)?		
Are my nails short and clean? Fingernails and toenails (if visible)?		
Have I remembered to remove any nail polish?		
Have I remembered to dispose of my chewing gum?		
Are my shoes clean?		
Is my uniform/workwear clean and pressed?		

with full flat shoes and socks, or a skirt with natural coloured tights. Again, it is a good idea to have two or more changes of clothes which you keep specially for work.

Professional appearance
Think about the clothes you wear to treat clients. Put yourself in your clients' shoes and imagine what sort of impression you make. Is that the kind of impression you want to make? Is it the right sort of impression?

'I saw a massage therapist in a hotel once when I was on holiday. He worked mainly on my back so I lay face down on the table with my face poking through a sort of hole. The massage was great, but the only problem was his feet. He was wearing sandals and he had these really horrible toenails – long and … well, I won't go into details. That's what I remember most about the session – having to stare down at his feet the whole time!'

Ashok

'Once I booked myself in for a morning's pampering at my health club – facial, nails, hair, the lot. Unfortunately, the woman who gave me a manicure stank of cigarettes. She must have popped out for a fag just before seeing me. Every time she turned her face towards me I got this whiff of stale smoke. Talk about ashtray breath! Ugh. I couldn't wait for the manicure to be over. That took the enjoyment away.'

Liz

YOUR PRACTICE ROOM
Your practice room is as important as your own appearance in helping clients to feel welcome and relaxed. The checklist above will help you consider the things you need to prepare well in advance of your appointments.

You should do everything you can to make your working surroundings pleasant for yourself and for your clients. A plant, a picture or some fresh flowers could make all the difference.

A professional workplace
Put yourself in your clients' shoes again and look carefully. What sort of impression does your workplace make? Are there any aspects of it that could be improved or made more welcoming? Be critical!

Checklist: Preparing your practice room	Yes	No
Do I have all the equipment I need?		
Is all the equipment in good working order?		
Do I have to hand all the supplies I need?		
Do I have enough spares or backups of everything?		
Are my working surroundings clean and hygienic?		
Is the environment attractive and comfortable?		
Are arrangements adequate for ensuring clients' modesty?		
Do I have my client's records/a new record card to hand?		
Is the environment safe for children – are there some toys available?		
Is my workplace clean and hygienic?		
Is it attractive and comfortable?		

'I have a wonderful hairdresser and I'd never go anywhere else, but one thing I can't stand is the music they have blaring in the background. Why do they always have to have loud pop music going on? I'm sure most of the customers don't want it. Anyway, it's mostly ladies of a certain age, like me. I've mentioned it once or twice, and they turn the music down, but next time I go it's back to the usual level.'

Shirley

END POINTS

- Professionalism means providing a service that clients are willing to put their trust in.
- Your appearance and mode of dress should give clients confidence in you.
- Your practice room should be welcoming, clean and comfortable.

Topic 1 looked at how to present yourself and your surroundings in a professional way. This topic goes on to look at other aspects of professionalism: time-keeping and working within the limits of your expertise.

BEING PUNCTUAL

'I waited ages at the clinic for my sports masseur to finish with her previous client. She apologised and said that she was running late. But it was the same every week – I always had to wait 15 or 20 minutes. Finally, I got sick of it and decided to try someone else.'

Stanley, footballer

Providing a professional service means giving a service that your clients can rely on. Keeping to time is an important part of this. If you do need to keep someone waiting for any reason, it is good manners to apologise.

If you find you are regularly running late, then you need to think about why this is and how you can change it.

- Are you drawing appointments out by chatting too much?

- Are you being over-generous with your time?

- Do you just forget to keep a watch on the clock?

- Are you underestimating how much you can do in a certain time?

- Do you need to build a 'handover' time into your appointments system?

'I put great value on punctuality. I've actually had clients say to me that they really like the fact that I run to schedule. They know that if they have an 11 o'clock appointment, that really means 11 o'clock, and they'll be away by 11.30.'

Charlie, physiotherapist

CANCELLATIONS

There will be times when you have to cancel appointments. Of course you should aim to avoid this whenever possible, as it causes disappointment and inconvenience to the client. However, occasionally it is unavoidable, through, e.g. illness, family crisis, powercuts or floods.

If you have to cancel an appointment, be as professional as possible.

- Let clients know as far in advance as possible.

- Make every effort to contact the client – leaving an answerphone message on their home phone will be no good if the client is at work. You could keep a note of mobile phone numbers.

- Always offer an alternative appointment for as soon as possible.

There will also be times when clients have to cancel. As you have set aside time for the client and may not be able to fill the appointment slot, this may mean a loss of income for you. On the other hand, clients may not want to pay for treatment they didn't receive.

Many practitioners operate a policy of making a charge if the cancellation is within 24 hours of the appointment time. Being professional means having a clear policy and making sure all clients are aware of it. Of course you can be flexible within this policy, i.e. not charge if a genuine emergency arises.

Your cancellation policy

What is your policy about missed or cancelled appointments?

How would you make clients aware of your policy?

You could include a statement about cancellations in a leaflet or information sheet you give to clients at the first appointment. You could also have a notice clearly visible in your practice room.

KNOWING YOUR ROLE AND ITS LIMITS

Another important part of professional conduct is knowing the limits of your expertise and staying within them. Remember that you are in a relationship of trust with your client. If you go beyond the limits of what you can or should do, you are breaking that trust.

Key Dos and Don'ts

Do:

• refer clients on to other professionals when necessary

• recommend only those treatments which are relevant and appropriate to the client.

Don't:

• offer advice or services outside the area in which you are qualified

• make false claims for the therapy you offer

• speak disrespectfully of other professionals.

Referring clients on

You should refer a client on if you find that you cannot help them, or that their problems are more serious than you had at first realised. The referral could be to a more experienced practitioner or, if appropriate, to a doctor or other healthcare provider. This is the professional course of action to take. Make sure you have the client's permission before passing on any details of their treatment and their health.

Staying within your limits

From time to time a client may ask – or you may feel tempted to offer – some advice in an area you are not qualified in. This could be dangerous both for your client and for you, should any harm come to the client as a result.

'I remember one client who used to come to me from time to time, mainly to work on his back and neck. One time he asked me to look at a mole on his leg that he thought was getting bigger – he was obviously worried about it. I think he just wanted me to say 'Oh, there's nothing to worry about', but I couldn't do that. What if I did and then it turned out to be cancerous? All I could do was advise him to see his doctor.'

Darren, masseur

Avoiding false claims

It is fine to say what you are aiming to do with your treatment or therapy, and what you hope might happen, but it is important not to make promises about the outcomes of your treatments.

If you make unrealistic or untrue promises, you are guaranteeing to disappoint the client when your promises fail to materialise.

You must also take great care not to say anything harmful about another therapist. Not only is it bad practice, but you could find yourself in court battling a case of libel.

END POINTS
- Good timekeeping is part of being professional.
- Avoid cancelling clients' appointments, but if you have to, handle it professionally.
- Be clear about your role – what you should and should not do.
- Refer clients on to other professionals when necessary.
- Never make promises or false claims about the treatment you offer.
- A professional therapeutic relationship is based on trust, empathy and mutual respect.

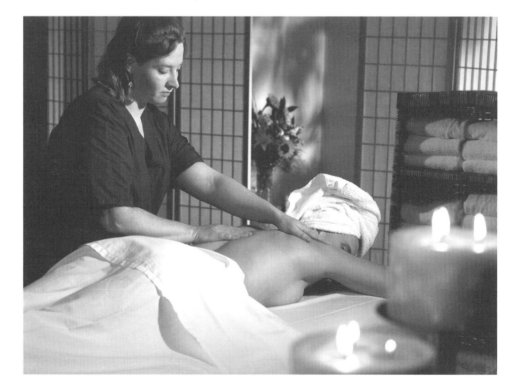

Topic 3 Keeping up to date

Your first professional qualification as a therapist is only the start of your professional development! In this topic you will look at why it is important to see training as a lifetime task. You will work out the benefits, and ways – formal and informal – of keeping up to date. You will also see that it is important to develop your business, not just your professional, skills.

WHY YOU NEED TO KEEP ON TRAINING

Imagine the situation: you have just finished a long course of study, you feel you've had enough training to last you a lifetime, you are raring to get stuck into your job and put into practice everything you have learnt. The last thing you want to hear is that you are just about ready for more training.

Most therapists, when they first start up in practice and are 'doing it for real', discover that they have more questions than answers – that their training has hardly prepared them for reality. This experience can be very daunting, but it is entirely normal.

The key point is that training is an ongoing, continuous process – something that you need to keep on doing throughout your professional life. Without continual updating, therapists very quickly become stale or out of touch with the latest developments in their field.

The term *continuing professional development* (CPD) is used to describe a way of thinking about work. It means that, as a professional, you understand that:

- your qualification is only the first stage of your learning

- it helps to belong to a professional community that is constantly striving to improve its standards
- it is vital to keep up to date with developments in your field
- you need to invest in yourself and your own learning.

Did you know…?
There are plans for some complementary therapies to come under statutory regulation, i.e. to be regulated by law, in the way that doctors, nurses and other health professionals are regulated (see Section 3 for more on regulation). If this happens, the professional associations of those therapies will be required to make certain undertakings, including committing its members to continuing professional development.

This will mean that, in order to remain registered, therapists will have to undertake a certain amount of training hours per year.

Most professional bodies require their members to obtain CPD points each year to remain on the register. There is a sample CPD Record in Section 5.

You might be interested in learning how to work with a particular client group – for example, children or people in hospital. Or you may want to learn more about a particular technique or preparation. You could, for example, look out for special courses put on by your professional association. You might approach a local school you know, or the human resources department in your local hospital, to express an interest.

WHAT KINDS OF TRAINING ARE RIGHT FOR ME?

There are two different ways of approaching your continuing professional development, and during your career you will probably want to do a mixture of both. They divide roughly into:

• informal learning (things that you can arrange for yourself)

• formal training (e.g. courses put on by your professional association, exhibitions and lectures).

Informal learning includes anything you do that broadens your knowledge, or increases your skill in your chosen area.

You might be surprised to see talks and evening classes mentioned in relation to your own professional development. But teaching things is a good way of learning.

Checklist: Types of informal learning

Read through the list and tick (in one colour) all the things that you already do towards your professional development. Then tick (in a different colour) everything else that would be relevant to you. Don't rule anything out! Add anything else that you do, or could do, to develop your skills. Highlight one activity that you would like to try out in the next six weeks.

Meeting with colleagues in your own therapy area to discuss issues related to your work	
Looking out for, and watching, television documentaries related to developments in your therapy area	
Reading the journal of your professional association on a regular basis	
Volunteering to give talks (e.g. at schools or local sports centres) on your therapy area	
Offering an evening class at your local further education college	
Keeping a learning journal	
'Sitting in' on consultations of more experienced practitioners (if appropriate for your therapy area)	
Working with a supervisor or mentor	

In teaching others you can:

- learn more about how members of the public see your chosen therapy
- refresh your memory about the theory, history and techniques of your chosen therapy
- gain a sense of pride in your work
- get insights into new areas you wish to work in.

IMPROVING YOUR BUSINESS SKILLS

If you want to run a successful business, it is not enough to be a good therapist. You also need to have good business skills. Section 1 contains information about the 'business' aspects of your business. If you employ other people, it is particularly important to hone your management and leadership skills. The Management and Leadership Council has devised a Business Improvement Tool which will help you to:

- think about how you are running your business, and
- identify areas for improvement.

The questionnaire is available to download from the Internet at www.managementandleadershipcouncil.org/bite/bite01.htm

KEEPING A PROFESSIONAL PORTFOLIO

One way of recording all your professional development activities is to keep a professional portfolio. This is just a record of all the things you do that contribute to remaining up to date with developments in your field and should include both formal and informal learning. You can keep cuttings and notes and copies of things you (or others) have written, as well as a list of courses you have attended,

books you have read, etc. There is a sample Continuing Professional Development (CPD) record card in Section 5 that you could use as the basis for your own portfolio. You should also contact your professional body for further information as professional portfolios are likely to gain a higher profile with the advent of statutory self-regulation.

Taking time out

In some professions where a lot of creative output is needed (for example teaching or the ministry), it is traditional to take a sabbatical after a few years (that is, a break of a few months or more). During this time the professional can rest from the demands of their usual job, to travel, research and follow up on things that really interest them.

Some complementary therapists also take sabbaticals after some time in practice, perhaps moving temporarily to work with a well-known practitioner whose work interests them, or to do something completely different for a while.

END POINTS

- All practitioners, no matter how experienced, need to grow and develop in their understanding of their work.
- It is vital to keep up to date with current developments; training is one way of doing this.
- It is important to plan for your own professional development – you can do this formally (through training) and informally (through activities you arrange yourself).
- If your therapy is one which is to come under statutory regulation, you may be obliged to undertake a programme of continuing professional development.

Topic 3 looked at the importance of keeping up to date with developments in your field of expertise. One of the best ways of learning and improving is simply by reflecting on your own experiences, with a view to learning from them. This topic looks at what it means to be a 'reflective practitioner'.

WHAT IS REFLECTION?

To reflect upon something means to consider it calmly and carefully. Reflection involves separating yourself from your experience so that you can examine and evaluate it.

Some people regard the ability to reflect as the hallmark of a professional, as opposed to someone who simply 'does their job'. People who are able to do this are known in the health care industry (and other places) as reflective practitioners.

'When a practitioner becomes a researcher into his own practice, he engages in a continuing practice of self-education.'

D. Schon (1991) The Reflective Practitioner

How people see the world

Most people, most of the time, don't look at things objectively. They perceive the world subjectively, from their own point of view.

You probably know that how you view events depends on:

- how you are feeling at the time
- what effect a particular event has on you
- your assumptions or opinions about what is going on
- a possible lack of understanding or knowledge.

All of these factors influence your view of reality and make it almost impossible for you to see things really clearly. It's a bit like seeing the whole world from one position. When you can stand back or, even better, stand higher, you get a much better view and can put things into perspective.

> **'Emotion recollected in tranquility': Wordsworth**
> Think of a recent incident at work or college that had an emotional effect on you.
>
> - How did you feel at the time?
> - How do you feel now? What has changed?
> - What have you learned from this incident?
> - Why was it critical in your professional development?

Time passes, and even a few days is enough time to calm down and see things more clearly. The incident itself hasn't changed, but you have.

When you realise that your perceptions are subjective, you have taken the first step to seeing things more clearly because you can allow for your own part in the process. This in turn helps you to see things from other points of view.

'We do not see things as they are but as we are.'

The Talmud

In essence, the practice of reflection is not difficult. It is likely that you are already doing it in your work, your studies and in your everyday life. The fact that you are reading this book indicates that you have given some thought to what you do well – or at least to what you don't do so well – and this is the basis of reflection.

WHY IS REFLECTION USEFUL?

As well as being the hallmark of a true professional, reflection is also one of the best ways of learning. The ability to see things clearly, to learn from your mistakes (and your successes), can help you in almost every area of life. You will become more able to respond appropriately and reasonably in any given situation, and more aware of other people's feelings and perceptions and the effects your actions have on other people. This can only be beneficial for your clients in terms of their own progress to fitness or health.

It can be difficult to recognise some of

your mental attitudes and assumptions because many of these are unconscious. Reflection can allow you to take a long, hard look at your actions and may reveal some interesting blind spots.

'May God give me the strength to change the things I can, the courage to accept the things I cannot change, and the wisdom to know the difference.'

Proverb

HOW TO DO IT

At its simplest, reflection is simply a way of monitoring how you are feeling at a given time.

> **Looking at your feelings**
> Draw cartoon faces to show:
>
> • how you felt at the end of your last day at work
>
> • how you felt the last time a client or colleague thanked you for something
>
> • how you are feeling at this moment.

Reflecting on your practice may not always be comfortable. You may discover things about yourself and the way you work that you do not like. If so, it is better to acknowledge the difficulty and how you feel about it, and try to put it right before other people realise it!

Sometimes, however, other people can recognise such things and help you acknowledge feelings and prejudices. It may also help to write things down – this is a good way of keeping track of changes, as you can look back and, hopefully, see how far you have come.

Critical incident analysis

There are several models of structured reflection. One of the first to be developed was critical incident analysis.

Many professionals, particularly in

Did **you know...?**

'Critical incident analysis is based on a procedure developed for recruiting pilots during World War II. It was based on a series of questions for flight instructors devised to reveal the most efficient (in this case, critical) behaviours.

Flanagan (1954)

healthcare, now use critical incident analysis to establish the most critical areas in their fields. The main aim is to establish:

- when you (or someone else) did something either effective or ineffective
- what led up to the incident
- exactly what happened
- why it was effective or ineffective
- what might be done differently another time.

Try this out for yourself.

Your own critical incident analysis
Think of an incident that has occurred during the last few days. It doesn't matter whether it was at home or at work – the main thing is to take some time to reflect on what happened.

- Briefly describe the incident: what happened?

- What did you do in response to the incident?

- Was the outcome satisfactory?

- If so, what did you do to contribute to the success?

- If not, what would you do differently next time?

'Reflecting has helped me change the way I do things. For example, I used to get impatient with some customers, especially ones who dithered about what they wanted. I'd get cool and distant, and could even be quite short with them. It wasn't good behaviour – and I always felt a bit cross with myself afterwards. I thought a lot about when it used to happen, and why. Finally I realised, with the help of a good friend, that, whatever the cause of the irritation (PMT,

difficulties at home, trouble with the car), the irritation was MY problem and much less to do with the client. I now feel much more aware of when I am irritated and can respond more constructively to the clients – after all, they might also be having a bad day!'

Jocelyne, hairdresser

END POINTS

- The ability to reflect on experience is one of the keys to being professional.
- Reflection offers the opportunity to learn more about yourself and, in turn, about others.
- Reflection involves looking calmly at an incident in an attempt to see clearly what was involved, so that you can behave differently another time.

This topic looks at the role of ethics in professional life. Ethics is simply to do with behaving in a decent and honourable way with your clients and colleagues. In order to define what is 'decent', professional associations publish guidelines or codes of ethics. This topic looks at why it is important to belong to a professional association and to know and follow their code of ethics.

WHY SHOULD I BELONG TO A PROFESSIONAL ASSOCIATION?

There are many different kinds of professional organisations. Some professional associations are set up for particular therapies/professions such as the Aromatherapy Organisations Council (AOC) where only aromatherapists are represented. Others such as the International Guild of Professional Practitioners represent multi-qualified therapists and these bodies are often members of the single therapy bodies.

Finding your professional association
Look in a copy of the Yellow Pages, and find the section called 'Reflexology'. Look for the boxed advertisements of the professional associations related to reflexologists.

Can you find the names of any other professional institutions or associations for other occupations, including your own?

Belonging to an association for your chosen area of work means that members of the public can have confidence in the service you provide. It tells potential clients that you are properly trained and that they have some protection if anything goes wrong with the treatment or service you provide.

Professional associations charge an annual fee for membership, and this will need to be budgeted for (see finance section). However, there are very many benefits to belonging to an association.

WHAT IS A CODE OF ETHICS?

Most professional organisations that train or license practitioners publish a document called a 'code of ethics', which all members must abide by. This defines the standards of behaviour that the organisation expects of its members. It ensures that they act in an honourable and professional manner.

Many of the rules in a code of ethics are based on common sense and decency. A code of ethics covers areas such as:

- the need for insurance

- relationships between practitioners – e.g. not enticing another practitioner's clients away from them

- not bringing the profession into disrepute

- relationships between clients and practitioners – e.g. most professional codes of conduct forbid any sexual contact between the client and the practitioner

Did you know...?

If you belong to a professional association you are entitled to use a form of letters after your name (e.g. ITEC) on your business cards, stationery and in any advertisements you place that show you are a member. You will also be able to hang your certificate of membership at your place of work, either in the reception area or in your practice room.

- behaving professionally – e.g. by not selling products that a client does not need
- complaints procedure for members of the public.

ITEC Code of Practice

You can find ITEC's own code of practice on its website at http://www.itecworld.co.uk/proff_intro.html It is also reproduced at the end of this book.

PROTECTING THE THERAPIST

The purpose of this code, as mentioned above, is to provide your clients with quality assurance. But it is also there to protect you.

In any field of work involved in dealing with people, whether these are clients, fellow practitioners, salon managers or members of the public, misunderstandings can arise. Knowing and understanding the code of ethics for your professional association will give you added protection in the event of a breakdown of communications.

'It can happen – rarely, thank God – that clients get angry or upset about something you do or don't do. I think some have unrealistic expectations, and not surprisingly, they end up getting disappointed. One bloke threatened "to report me", and get me "struck off", claiming I'd acted "unprofessionally", but I was confident I'd followed the guidelines. I explained calmly to him that he was entitled to contact the relevant body, but also explained that I had followed their guidelines to the letter – which I think he knew really. In the end he calmed down and apologised.'

Tony, physiotherapist

In Topics 1 and 2, which deal with 'professionalism', you learnt that there should be a bond of trust between a client and a practitioner. There is a lot that you can do to cultivate this trust with your clients, and the topics in this section are designed to help you to do this. For example, you can:

- develop your communication skills (see Topics 11 to 14)
- ensure that you adhere to client confidentiality (see Topic 6)
- learn how to deal with feedback positively (see Topic 14).

These things will help you maintain good relationships with your clients, and everyone you come into contact with through your work.

Checking your code of ethics
Make sure you have a copy of the code of ethics for the professional association to which you belong. Take it out and look at the areas it covers. If there is anything you don't understand, you could ask your supervisor (if you have one), a more experienced practitioner in your field, or phone your professional association for guidance.

END POINTS

Belonging to your professional association and adhering to its code of conduct ensures that:

- potential clients know that you are properly qualified for the service you provide
- practitioners in other therapies can refer clients to you with confidence
- you have some protection if communications break down with a client or fellow practitioner.

As a professional therapist, you have to understand what it means to act ethically. Two important aspects of ethical behaviour are maintaining confidentiality and seeking consent when necessary. This topic looks in turn at each of these.

WHAT DOES CONFIDENTIALITY MEAN?

'While my homoeopath was on maternity leave, she referred me to a locum. I was worried about all the personal things I had told her about myself being read by another person. She assured me that my file would be kept confidential, and that she would only pass on to the locum a one-page summary of the remedies I had had. When I arrived for my first consultation with the locum, I was horrified to find my full file open on his desk. I felt extremely exposed, and my relationship with my homoeopath never really recovered.'

Margaret, homoeopathic client

When is a secret not a secret?
Think about a time – perhaps when you were a child – when you told a secret to someone, and that person broke your trust by talking about it to someone else. How did you feel?

Confidentiality means that a client can trust you not to reveal their personal details to any other person. The kind of information you hold on your clients will depend on the kind of work you do. If you are an aromatherapist, you will probably need more information about your client than, say, a hairdresser normally would. It also depends on the client and how much or how little they want to say about themselves.

As a complementary therapist, it is not acceptable to reveal anything that a client

has told you – either about their illnesses or about their personal lives – to any other person without their express permission.

This means not discussing information about them with anyone, including:

- friends and family
- other clients
- other therapists at your place of work
- their GP (without the client's consent).

'I know that's a secret, for it's whispered everywhere!'

Congreve

Clients are more likely to trust you if they are sure that what they tell you will remain confidential. This, in turn, has a positive effect on the treatment or service you offer them, and the loyalty they will have to you.

Keeping notes confidential
Keeping confidentiality also applies to any notes you take in consultations with your clients. If you do keep a record of any kind of personal information, you should store your files in a secure box or filing cabinet under lock and key. You can find out more about keeping notes and records in Section 1.

Did **you know…?**

Some practitioners like to assure clients of their policy on confidentiality before undertaking any treatment. You can mention it:

- at the beginning of your first consultation with a client

- in your brochures or any advertising material you put out.

Being security conscious
Spend a few minutes thinking about the system you use for maintaining client records. How secure is it? Are there any times when people other than you might be able to see records about clients (e.g. do you ever leave your room empty with records on your desk?).

When can you discuss information about a client?

There are a very few occasions when you may need to disclose information about a client. These circumstances include the following situations.

- Your client is under 16 years old and child protection legislation applies. Note that parental consent is required to treat a minor and parents should be given the opportunity to remain in the room during treatment.

- You need to check out with a GP whether it is safe to treat a person. In this case, you should seek the client's permission to approach their GP.

- You suspect serious professional misconduct on the part of another professional. Again, you would normally seek your client's permission before taking the matter further.

- You want to use a client's details as part of your own supervision. Certain therapies require that practitioners have regular supervision with more experienced practitioners. In order to do this, you may need to share details of clients' illnesses/personal history with the supervisor. The normal practice, however, is for the details to be discussed, but for the client's identity to remain confidential. Again, it is good practice to ask the client's permission before taking supervision on their case.

The General Medical Council's *Blue Book* lists the following circumstances in which it is considered acceptable to break confidentiality:

- where the patient has given his/her consent to the nature and extent of disclosure

- in an emergency or other dangerous situation where, in the opinion of the practitioner, the information may assist in the prevention of possible injury to the patient or to another

- where notification to the appropriate authority of a notifiable disease or food poisoning is required, unless s/he has reasonable grounds for believing that a registered medical practitioner has already done so

- where a court has ordered disclosure

- disclosure in the public interest, e.g. a situation in which failure to disclose appropriate information would expose the patient or someone else to a risk of death or serious harm

- with the patient's consent, sharing information with other health professionals on a 'need to know' basis (only pass on what is relevant).

WHAT DOES CONSENT MEAN?

Under most circumstances, a client is considered to consent to treatment you offer if you have discussed and agreed a course of treatment and the client then presents themselves for an appointment with you.

There are some occasions, however, when you will need to obtain written consent before you start a course of treatment with a client. You may need to have the client's written consent, or sometimes the consent of a third person.

Checklist: Gaining consent

Is my client...

1	under 16 years of age? (Working with children requires you to comply with The Children Act)
2	too ill to consent themselves (for example, an unconscious adult)?
3	taking prescribed medication from a General Practitioner?
4	suffering from any medical conditions that might contraindicate treatment?

Informed consent, represented by a signature (witnessed and dated by the therapist), is more legally binding and should happen before every treatment. In most cases, therapists and salons do not insist on this, but in the event of a lawsuit, this could make the difference between fighting a court case on your own, and having the support of your professional body. The checklist at the top of the page will help you decide when you may need to get consent from someone other than the client.

If you answered 'yes' to any of these questions, you will need to seek the consent from someone other than the client.

1 You will need written consent from a parent or guardian to carry out any treatment.

2 You will need consent from a guardian or next of kin.

3 You should seek the GP's consent (with the agreement of your client). Not all prescribed medication contraindicates other treatment, but you will need to check to be safe.

4 Again, you should seek the GP's consent. This should take the form of a letter or tear-off form with an SAE. Make sure you have a copy for the client and a copy for your records. See the sample included in Section 5.

For more information on contraindications, see Topic 10.

END POINTS

• To work ethically and professionally, you need to understand and maintain client confidentiality. You also need to recognise situations when consent is required.

• Confidentiality applies to all personal information about a client. This includes both information you have asked for and information clients choose to confide in you.

• There are a few situations where you may discuss a client's personal information or treatment details – be sure that you know what these are.

• Written records with clients' personal details must be kept under lock and key.

Complementary therapies are primarily about working with people. For this reason, knowing how to create and maintain good relationships is essential for anyone wanting to work in this field.

This is the first of three topics looking at relationships. This topic is a general introduction to the relationships you will have as a complementary therapist. Topics 8 and 9 look at working with other therapists and the medical profession.

WHO DO YOU RELATE TO?

A successful practice depends on good relationships with many people, but particularly with:

- clients
- fellow practitioners in your own field and in other fields
- the community in which you practise.

Imagine your business as a bicycle wheel with yourself at the hub. The spokes are

Checklist: Who do you relate to?

Use this checklist to make a quick survey of all the different kinds of people you are likely to relate to as part of your work. You can use the blank spaces at the end of our list to add others you can think of.

Clients

Practice manager (if working from a practice)

Practice receptionist (if working from a practice)

Therapists in the same field

Therapists in different fields

The client's care team

Supervisor

Suppliers/servicers of equipment and product companies

Members of the public

Bank manager

Cleaners

Your family members (particularly if working from home)

Doctors

Accountant

Tax office

Professional organisation

the relationships that make the wheel turn – and keep your practice going. You will need to relate to different kinds of people in your chosen field.

You may be surprised at the range of different relationships you have.

Some of these people you will see every day; others only every week or every month. Some you will see only rarely (such as your accountant, if you have one) – perhaps only once a year.

The daily relationships are probably the ones you work at most, but all these relationships need to be maintained. For example, communicating effectively with your accountant or bank manager can not only save you time and hassle when it comes to filling out tax returns, it can save you money!

'My practice room is in a health centre, where lots of other therapists work, together with some medical staff. Although I give most of my energy to my clients, I am aware that the centre has a spider's web of relationships and it's important to devote a bit of energy to those. A few friendly words with the receptionists each day, for example, helps to keep the wheels oiled! I make a point of chatting to the other therapists when I can, and can safely say I'm on good terms with everyone working here – including the contract cleaners who catch me working late on my accounts!'

Mel, herbalist

WHAT IS A GOOD WORKING RELATIONSHIP?

The basis of good working relationships, like any relationship, is mutual respect and good communication (see Section 2, Topics 11 to 16). However, as a complementary practitioner you have particular responsibilities to:

- your clients – this is covered in more depth in Topics 11 to 15
- your fellow practitioners – see Topic 8
- other medical practitioners such as GPs – dealt with in Topic 9.

A bit of appreciation
Can you remember the last time someone thanked you for a piece of work that you had done well? How did you feel?

Can you remember the last time you thanked someone else?

'It took a lot of patience to sort out my client's problem. There were times when we both wanted to give up. But at the end she wrote me such a nice note thanking me for all my trouble, it made it all feel worthwhile!'

Aileen, counsellor

A bit of appreciation can go a long way in creating good working relationships, and means that when you do run into difficulties, you will have a good basis of trust to work from.

END POINTS
- A successful practice depends on good relationships with many people.
- The most important relationship is that with the client, but you also need to work with other therapists and practitioners, suppliers and the wider community.
- The basis of good working relationships is mutual respect and good communication.

Many people working as therapists, whether in practice or on their own, have some kind of association or contact with other therapists. This topic looks at good and bad ways of developing relationships with other therapists.

PROFESSIONAL BOUNDARIES

The key to good working relationships with other therapists is having good professional boundaries. What does this mean? In a nutshell, it means knowing exactly what you can and cannot do, and working to these limits, while at the same time respecting the work of other therapists.

Everyone has a version of the tale of the builder who comes round to give a quote for some work on a house and shakes their head, saying: 'Don't know who did this for you, madam – must have been real cowboys. I'll have to rip it out and start again…'

Talking in this way about other therapists or salons is poor practice. For a start, it is not likely to impress the customer or client, as they will probably see through the ploy. It may make them suspicious of you.

'I have a vivid memory of sitting in the barber's chair in my teens and this man fiddling with my hair saying "Who on earth made this mess? Did your mother cut your hair?". It really annoyed me. I wanted to say "How dare you be so rude?" Yes, it probably was my mum, because we couldn't afford for me to have my hair cut.'

Alice

Criticising fellow practitioners is neither professional nor ethical. People who do this are stepping beyond their professional boundaries. True professionals do not need to make others look bad in order to make themselves look good. If you believe in your own good work, let it speak for itself.

Clients may volunteer stories about bad experiences they have had with other therapists. However, it is wise not to join in with the criticism. You weren't present, so how can you comment?

An exception to this rule is if there are Child Protection issues involved, or if you suspect serious professional misconduct on the part of a fellow therapist. In these cases, you cannot ignore the possibility of behaviour that could be abusive and/or criminal. You should encourage your client to report the incident to the relevant professional association. It is quite likely that your professional code of practice has some guidelines on this matter.

'If we believe that a child we are treating is at risk, we have a professional duty to bring this to the attention of the Child Protection Officer at our local social services department.'

From the Society of Homeopaths Code of Ethics and Practice

Cultivating good relationships

There are, of course, many positive aspects to having good relationships with other therapists in your area, especially for those just starting out in practice.

Getting to know you

Think about how you might get to know other therapists in your area. If you were to write a letter introducing yourself, what might you say?

Cultivating good relationships with others in your field, and letting them know your areas of interest and specialities, can mean that you:

- may get referrals from more established therapists who are too busy to see new clients, or who know that you offer a particular service their client needs
- have a pool of colleagues you trust, to whom you can refer clients
- have a supportive network of fellow therapists to turn to for advice on particular matters
- will get to hear of new developments in your field that might benefit you or your clients.

KNOWING YOUR LIMITATIONS

Just as it is inappropriate to 'talk down' the services of others, so it is unethical – and just plain bad business – falsely to 'talk up' your own services or products. The ITEC Code of Practice, for example, deals specifically with not making claims for a service or a product that have not been proved to be true.

There is no shame in being clear with a client about what you can and can't help them with. Referring a client on to another suitable practitioner lets the client know that you take their safety and well-being seriously. It can enhance your professional image and show them that you take a broad view of their needs, rather than a narrow one.

Referrals might be appropriate in the following situations.

- If you are too busy to see a client within a reasonable time-frame, you can offer them the option of seeing a colleague. They may choose to do this if they want to be seen urgently, or they may choose to wait to see you.
- If you suspect that your client has underlying emotional problems hindering their recovery, you should refer them to a counsellor.
- If you suspect that your client has a serious underlying medical condition, you should refer them to their GP. In some cases (about which your professional association can advise you), you will need their GP's permission to treat the patient. This is covered more fully in Topic 10.

END POINTS

- The key to good working relationships with other therapists is having good professional boundaries.
- Criticising fellow practitioners is poor practice. It is unethical and unprofessional, and the client is likely to see through the ploy.
- Avoid being drawn into criticising fellow practitioners.
- If you suspect serious professional misconduct on the part of a fellow therapist, you should then encourage the client to report the incident.
- Cultivating good relationships with others in your field can have many benefits, in terms of referrals, support and friendship.
- It is unethical – and just plain bad business – falsely to 'talk up' your own services or products.

This topic looks at ways of developing relationships with members of the medical profession. For some complementary therapists, this will be an important part of their work, partly because of the need to refer clients and partly to offer services that may benefit GPs' patients. It is good practice to correspond with the patient's GP with the patient's consent and may also help to establish your practice in the area.

TALKING TO THE MEDICAL PROFESSION

A chance to say your piece
Imagine that you are invited to address a gathering of GPs in your area for five minutes about the therapy you offer. What would you want to say to them?

Your response to this invitation will depend on many things – such as how confident you feel about talking in public, and how easy or difficult you find it to explain things that you know 'in your own head' to other people.

It can also be a big challenge to talk to people who may be sceptical about your chosen field – and, though attitudes are changing fast, you will encounter a range of attitudes to your work among the medical profession. Some fully accept the value of complementary therapies for improving people's health and well-being; others take a narrower view, regarding medical interventions as the only useful ones.

'Some of the GPs are great, but with others, it does feel a bit like banging your head against a brick wall, but I've learned to develop a thick skin. It helps to be confident in what you do. I know the value of my therapy to clients and I'm not going to be put off by other people's narrow-mindedness.'
Gareth, Alexander Technique teacher

As a complementary practitioner, it is important to take a positive, proactive and professional approach to developing relationships with doctors in your area.

BEING POSITIVE
Being comfortable about explaining to people what you do, and why, will help you develop good relationships with other practitioners (complementary or medical). You might find this difficult to begin with, but practice will help enormously. You may even find you enjoy it!

'Tell me about what you do'
Working with a friend, or with a tape recorder, practise talking about what you do and why you do it.

BEING PROACTIVE
Unless you are employed by a GP practice or in a hospital, it will be up to you to make contact with the medical professionals in your area. You may choose to wait until you need to refer a client, or you can take the initiative in letting them know that you are there.

Checklist: Points to cover in a 'briefing' about your therapy

You might talk about any of these points. Use the blank spaces at the bottom to add in anything else that you think is relevant.

Why you have come to see them (e.g. 'I have just started up in practice and I wanted to make myself known to you.')	
The name of your therapy, and where you practise	
What a consultation involves	
The name of the professional association you belong to	
How your therapy works/ what it aims to do – three sentences	
What the main benefits of the therapy are (if you can talk from your own experience, so much the better, e.g. 'Patients usually tell me that they feel more relaxed after a treatment') – three points	
Something about yourself (e.g. where you live, how long you have been in practice, why you wanted to train in this area) – three points	

Did you know...?

You can get a list of GPs in your postcode area from the NHS web site on **www.NHS.uk**. Select the 'local services' box in the right hand corner of the home page, and select the 'GP surgeries' option. You can then enter the postcode (or part postcode) of the area you are interested in and get a list of addresses and phone numbers.

You could:

- write a letter to introduce yourself. You can use the points in the checklist above as a guide. If you word-process the letter, you can use the same text, 'topping and tailing' each with the name of the individual doctor and your signature. Later in this section, we will look in more detail at writing letters. See also the sample introductory letter in Section 5.

- send (or take) a copy of the advertisement announcing the opening of your practice or salon, or your practice information sheet (if you plan to prepare one) to the GP practices in your area.

BEING PROFESSIONAL

You may feel that going to the trouble of contacting medical practitioners in your area is a fairly low priority – especially if you are just starting up in practice. However, consider these points.

- If you need to refer a client to a GP, or ask the GP's permission to treat a client, this will be very much easier if the lines of communication are already open. It takes time to build good relationships. Why not start now, when you may have a little extra time on your hands?

- Taking the initiative will build up your confidence, and help you feel established in a new area.

- This is your chance to be an ambassador for your chosen therapy! You have invested time and effort in training, and believe in what you do. Take the opportunity to let those in the medical profession who may not know about your therapy know what you can offer.

Sharing information

In some areas there are special forums where members of the medical profession interested in complementary therapies, and practitioners from different therapies, can discuss areas of common interest. This is a good way to meet sympathetic GPs. Find out from your local library or complementary therapy clinic whether there is one operating in your area.

You will look at the issue of competence and contraindictions in the next topic.

END POINTS

- For some complementary therapists, working with the medical profession will be an important part of their work.

- Some medical professionals fully accept the value of complementary therapies for improving people's health and well-being; others take a more sceptical view. You have to learn to deal with both.

- Be prepared to take the initiative in making relationships with GPs in your area: find out about practices, make contacts, join relevant organisations and forums.

- Let GPs know that you are a professional who understands the importance of working within your area of competence.

- Be confident about your area of therapy and its benefits.

If you notice something that causes you concern when you are treating a client – a physical problem or something about the client's behaviour – you may ask yourself whether it's safe to carry on treating the client. The main question is whether carrying on the treatment is likely to harm the client or whether harm may arise if the patient is not referred to a GP or accident and emergency department. This topic looks at situations like these and what to do in them.

WHAT ARE CONTRA-INDICATIONS?

The kinds of contraindications that you will need to be aware of will be dictated by the kind of therapy that you practise.

Your list of contraindications

Under what circumstances would you not feel safe in proceeding with a treatment for a client? List as many different contraindications as you can think of.

You will have learned about contraindications specific to the kind of therapy you practise during your professional training course. If you are unsure about what these are, you should obtain an up-to-date list from your professional association. You may find it helpful to pin up a list of 'red flag' symptoms (see page 101) in your treatment room to remind yourself of the really serious danger signals.

A helpful way to remember contraindications is to classify them into three different types. Contraindications can be:

1 total – your client has a condition which makes it unsafe for you to treat them

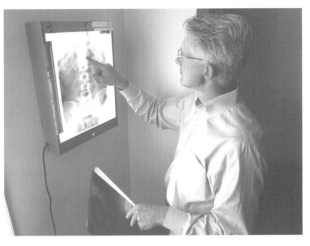

2 localised (relevant to a therapy such as massage) – your client has a condition that makes it unsafe for you to massage or manipulate a particular part of their body, but you can massage or treat safely other, unaffected parts

3 medical – you can treat the client after you have obtained medical permission.

As an example, contraindications for massage therapy are listed in the three different areas in the chart on the following page.

As you can see, there is some overlap between the categories, and you will need to make some judgements about what is safe and what is not safe. For example, athlete's foot could be classified as a 'skin disease', but very few medical practitioners would consider it unsafe to massage somebody's back or neck because they had athlete's foot (although you would want to make sure that the feet had not been touched and that you wash your hands before and after treatment!).

Making these kinds of judgements is particularly hard when you are starting out as a practitioner – err on the side of caution and take advice from someone more experienced.

Total	Local	Medical
Therapist should not massage if client is/has:	*Therapist cannot massage areas affected by:*	*Massage only after approval by a GP in cases of:*
fever	undiagnosed lumps and bumps	pregnancy
contagious or infections diseases	varicose veins	cardio-vascular conditions (thrombosis, phlebitis, hypertension, hypotension, pacemaker, angina, circulatory problems)
under the influence of drugs or alcohol	bruising	any condition already being treated by a medical practitioner
behaving aggressively or irrationally and you feel in danger from the client	cuts/abrasions	any condition already being treated by another complementary therapy practitioner
	sunburn	oedema
	undiagnosed pain	diabetes
	inflammation	cancer
making you feel sexually threatened		nervous or psychotic conditions
e.g. suicidal or very 'needy', so that you feel 'out of your depth'.		nervous system disorders: epilepsy, Bell's palsy, trapped or pinched nerves

Source: Adapted from An Introductory Guide to Massage *by Louise Tucker*

The reason why

It is much easier to remember the contraindications for therapy if you know why it is not safe to treat the person. For each of the contraindications in the therapy you practise, try to work out why it would be unsafe to treat a client with that condition.

The reason for some contraindications is fairly obvious, e.g. a massage therapist would not attempt to massage any area of a client's body that is badly sunburned, or where there is a deep cut or bruise, for fear of causing more damage to the area and pain to the client.

Other contraindications require a deeper knowledge of the body and disease processes, for example:

- infections: there may be a danger of spreading the infection to other parts of the patient's body, or of catching it yourself
- skin conditions: these may be inflamed by the use of oils and friction
- cancer: therapies such as massage encourage lymph drainage. In some cases there may be a danger of a client's cancer spreading through the lymphatic system.

Note that cancer is an area requiring specialist knowledge and is a growth area for treatment within palliative care.

Specific contraindications

For clients who are allergic to certain substances, those particular substances will obviously be contraindicated in any treatment you offer.

Bear in mind that the aim of your practice is to increase your client's sense of well-being. Adapt your treatment to their needs.

'Red flag' symptoms and notifiable diseases

You need to be able to recognise 'red flag' symptoms and know how quickly to refer clients, and to whom. Obvious 'red flag' symptoms include:

- high fever, especially if in conjunction with a rash, stiff neck, sensitivity to light, vomiting, delirium
- very high (or very low) blood pressure
- frequent coughing, especially coughing up blood.

You should also be aware of notifiable diseases. Keep a complete list of these (this should be available from your professional organisation) and if you suspect that a patient has any of the signs or symptoms associated with any of these diseases, you should:

- encourage your patient to seek a diagnosis from their own GP as soon as possible; record this on the notes
- contact your local Environmental Health Officer for further advice and record this in the notes.

ETHICAL DIMENSIONS

Some of the contraindications in the table above have an ethical dimension to them. These include:

1 situations where, in addition to a potential danger to the client, there is also a danger to you, including situations where:

  - you feel in danger from the client (they are behaving aggressively or irrationally)
  - you feel sexually threatened by the client
  - you feel 'out of your depth' with the client, e.g. the client is suicidal or very 'needy'. (You will need to rely on your 'gut feeling' about whether a situation is safe. If you are in any doubt, seek advice.)

2 situations where you need to observe professional boundaries – this applies where your client is already being treated by another practitioner, whether a medical practitioner or another complementary therapist. If you are unsure, you should always ask the client's permission to approach the practitioner first. If you already know them, you can do this by telephone, if not, you may prefer to write.

Did **you know**…?

If you are unsure about your safety when treating a client, you can arrange for a colleague to stay within earshot during the consultation. Some women therapists do not treat male clients from home if they are alone in the house during practice hours.

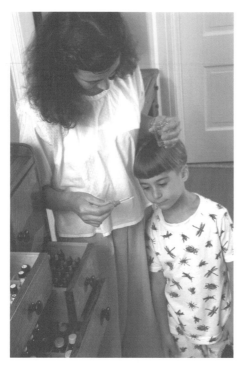

END POINTS

- A contraindication is any factor in a patient's condition that makes it unwise to pursue a certain line of treatment.

- Make sure you are familiar with the contraindications for your particular kind of therapy.

- You will remember them better if you understand the reason for the contraindication. You might find it useful to make yourself a chart to keep with you during your consultations with clients.

- Contraindications are sometimes a matter of judgement. It takes practice to know when to refer and when to take medical advice. Be patient with yourself while you learn!

- If uncertain, do not treat.

Topic 11 Communicating with clients (1): introduction

As a complementary health practitioner, relating well to people is an essential part of your business. Communication skills are at the heart of your ability to relate to clients. Since communication is a two-way process, to communicate effectively with clients and colleagues you must also encourage them to communicate well with you.

There are four topics in this section that deal with communication. This topic is an introduction to communication, and looks specifically at asking questions. The following three topics look at listening skills, body language and giving and receiving feedback.

THAT'S A GOOD QUESTION!

Asking questions is one of the best ways of encouraging clients to communicate with you – to give you the information you need to treat them effectively.

Open and closed questions
There are two kinds of questions.

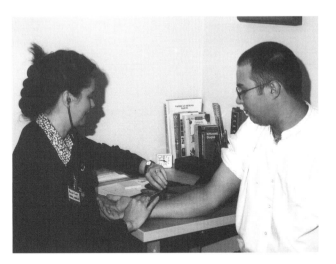

- **Closed questions** are those to which your client will be able to give a short, factual answer, or say 'yes' or 'no'. For example, 'Does that hurt?' is a closed question.

- **Open questions** can't be answered with a 'yes' or a 'no'. They invite your client to say something about themselves, their feelings, their experiences, their ideas. 'What sort of pain is it?' is an open question, because it invites the person to answer in more detail.

Closed question	Open question
'Have you had massage/reflexology treatment/aromatherapy before?'	'How can I help you?' or 'What do you hope the treatment will do for you?'
'You have made this appointment because you have trouble sleeping. Is that right?'	'Tell me about how you sleep.'
'Do you eat healthy food?'	'Tell me about your diet.'
'Are you worried about this treatment?'	'What are your worries about having this treatment?'

Generally speaking, closed questions are useful for situations in which you need factual information, such as name, address and phone number. When you need to know how a client feels, what they think,

what their experience is, you will need to ask an open question.

Some examples of different types of question are listed below.

As these examples show, it is important to

be aware of the type of question you are asking, and to avoid asking a closed question when an open question would be more useful.

Open questions are particularly useful in the following situations:

- in your first consultation with a client, particularly when you are taking their history and filling in the client record card

(For more information on the client record card, see Section 1, Topic 13. You will look in more detail at the first consultation in Section 2, Topic 15.)

- whenever you need to check with clients about the treatment you are giving. You will look in more depth at giving and receiving feedback in Section 2, Topic 14.

Open questions can also help to bring a more productive atmosphere to any heated discussion or situation of conflict you may find yourself in as a practitioner, whether with clients, a clinic or salon manager, or colleagues. These might be questions such as:

- What would you like me to do?
- What are the different options you are thinking about?
- What would be the benefits of doing that?
- How do you feel about that?

BEING COMFORTABLE WITH SILENCE

It may seem strange, but a key communication skill is being able to be comfortable in silence. Many people feel uncomfortable when they are alone with another person they don't know well. The instinct may be to 'reach out' to them in some way and fill the gap with conversation.

Once you have established a good rapport with a client, and have all the information you need, you should be very wary indeed of introducing other topics of conversation. If you have you ever had an experience of a professional such as a cab driver, hairdresser or storekeeper who just wouldn't stop talking, you will know what it feels like to be a 'captive audience'.

How you feel about people telling you their opinions or experiences will depend on how you feel that day, and on your situation. If you have a few minutes to spare, you may not mind hearing about the customer who came into the shop before you, but if you are on your way to a difficult meeting or a funeral, you will probably prefer the opportunity to gather your thoughts in silence.

Generally speaking, it is not appropriate to open conversations with a client on anything other than what you need to say. This is because:

- your client is paying for this time with you; you need to focus on their needs
- your client may give extra weight to what you say, because of your professional role in relation to them; what to you is a casual remark may be taken very seriously by them
- you may risk offending your client; if your opinions do not match theirs, it puts them in a very difficult position during your treatment time.

In some cases, clients may open a topic of conversation, and usually it is fine for you to respond, as long as you are able to focus fully on what you are doing during the treatment. However, take care that your client doesn't feel uncomfortable 'taking up your time' or that they need to 'entertain' you during the session.

You will need to know the difference between situations in which some enjoyable small talk helps the patient, and situations where silence is more appropriate. With some therapies, silence is an important part of the treatment, as it helps the client to relax and enjoy the full benefits of your skill.

'With new clients, I tell them that I work in silence and that they should enjoy the relaxation that they will experience. At the same time, I encourage them to tell me if they feel pain or discomfort when I'm working on any part of the foot, as it's important for me to know that.'

Anne, reflexologist

END POINTS

- As a complementary health practitioner, relating well with people is an essential part of your business. Communication skills are at the heart of your ability to relate to clients.

- Asking questions is one of the best ways of encouraging clients to communicate with you. Open questions encourage clients to give more information than closed ones.

- A key communication skill is being comfortable with silence, especially when silence is part of the therapy.

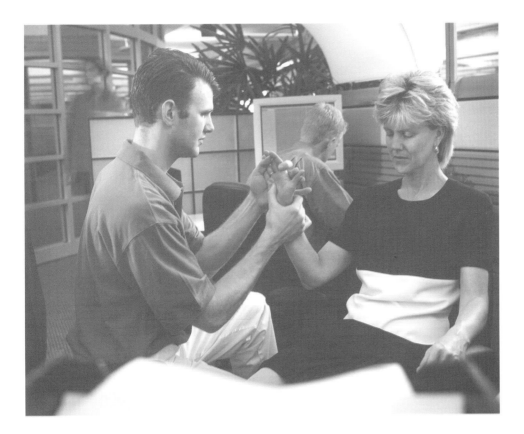

Many people think that good communication is all about being able to speak clearly and express yourself well. Those are important aspects of communication, but it's just as important to listen well. Sometimes listening is the best thing you can do to relate well with clients. This topic looks at why good listening is important and what it involves.

ARE YOU REALLY LISTENING?

'I wanted to get my hairdresser's attention to tell him that he was cutting my hair too short, but he kept laughing and having a private joke with his colleague. I didn't know how to interrupt their banter. I left feeling really angry that I had spent so much money on a haircut that I didn't like.'

Min

'The sports therapist asked me what I wanted from my workout programme. I hesitated because I was a bit shy, and she sighed and said, really loudly, "Is it weight loss? Muscle tone? Strength training?" She seemed really impatient. I didn't have the courage to tell her that I needed exercises that would help me keep my bones healthy now that I have had the menopause. I felt so stupid.'

Christine

'The reflexologist never really looked at me. She asked me a lot of questions, but she kept her eyes on the chart in front of her. I got the feeling she wasn't very interested in what I was saying, so after a while I stopped really trying to explain how I felt and I never told her that I had been feeling really tired since my father died six months ago.'

Jack

> **A good listener**
> Why do you think it is necessary to be a good listener in your role as a complementary therapist?

To ensure that your clients get the correct treatment, you need to:

- get correct information from your client – the client with the bad haircut is unlikely to go back to the hairdresser who ignored his wishes or to recommend any of his friends to that salon

- get enough detail about the background and health of your client to ensure that you offer the correct treatment – the sports therapist in the second quote failed to discover what her client needed from her exercise programme

- ensure that your client feels able to confide in you where necessary – the attitude of the reflexologist in the third situation meant that she lost an important opportunity to empathise with her client. She also missed important information about the reason for her client's symptoms.

Being a good listener also helps to build up trust between you and your client, which will have a good effect on your client's well-being and on your enjoyment of your job. It also makes it easier for you to talk to your client about areas which might be difficult – for example, if you have to suggest a lifestyle change which you know will be difficult for them. A client who feels that you listen to them and care about them is more likely to follow any advice you give them.

WHAT MAKES A GOOD LISTENER?

A better listener
Look again at the three examples given on the opposite page. How would you advise each of three therapists to become a better listener?

The hairdresser could improve his listening skills by keeping his attention focused on his client, rather than his colleagues, so that clients do not feel ignored. He could also check in with his client by asking questions; for example, 'When you said you wanted an inch off, did you mean all round, or just at the back?'.

Instead of butting in before her client had had time to answer the question, the sports therapist should have shown more

patience and used a smile or a nod to encourage her client to say what she needed from her treatment. She might also have encouraged her by saying, quietly, 'Perhaps you are not sure yet of what you want. Would you like me to explain the different kinds of programme we offer?' This would have helped the client to feel valued and might have encouraged her to say what she needed.

Like many therapists, the reflexologist needs to refer to, and to fill in the client record card when interviewing her client. However, she should be sure to make eye contact with the client while the client is speaking. When she is sure that the client has said all she needs to say, the therapist can say, 'I would like to make a note of that.'

Really good listeners try to listen to what lies behind the words the other person is saying. This requires considerable concentration but is well worth the effort.

'The gift of profound listening is among the most difficult to give and the most beneficial to receive.'

Dr Marty Nemko

END POINTS
Good listening skills include:

• being focused on your client for the time they are with you and making them feel important – that is what they are paying you for!

• offering your client encouragement to speak – sometimes you might need to ask them another question, to show that you are really interested in their answer

• making eye contact while your client is speaking to you

• remembering things clients say so you can ask them questions at the next appointment about their family/job/ interests.

Did you know...?

Many people feel better just by being able to confide in someone who will not judge them. Not having anyone to confide in can affect a person's mental health adversely.

Did you know...?

When a client hesitates before answering a question, it is usually because they are trying to decide whether to tell you something important. Remember to give them time and encouragement.

Body language is a surprisingly important part of the communication skills you use with your clients. According to some estimates, it makes up more than half of what you 'say' to your client.

This topic looks at how you can use body language in a positive way to improve communication with clients. It also examines how you can learn more about what your clients are feeling and thinking by being aware of their body language.

Look again at the third quote at the start of Topic 12: here, a reflexologist's poor body language – her failure to make eye contact with her client – causes her to miss an important symptom.

Doing the wrong thing
Think of a time when you have been intimidated by a professional, such as a GP or a lawyer. What did that person do that made you feel unimportant, frightened or threatened?

'I went to the solicitor to talk about my separation from my partner. I had thought that I was doing OK until she looked at me from behind her desk, and said 'What can I do for you?'. When I started to cry she got up, and came and sat next to me. It was much easier to talk to her there.'

Alison

The client can also get a bad feeling if the professional:

• does not take the time to come and meet and greet the client politely

• keeps the client waiting without apologising

• talks to them from behind a huge desk

• never looks up from their notes

• drums their fingers on the desk or looks out of the window while the client is talking

• sits with their arms crossed.

Body language is especially important in therapies where clients have to remove clothing, as they are particularly vulnerable in this situation. It should go without saying that a therapist should never do anything that makes a client feel uncomfortable.

'I had to take off my shirt, so the osteopath could treat my stiff neck and shoulders. Whenever I looked at him, he seemed to be looking at my breasts. I just could not relax throughout the whole treatment and decided to go to his female colleague the next time I needed treatment.'

Dawn

The good news is, that with a little practice, it is easy to use positive body language to make your clients feel comfortable.

Doing the right thing
Think of all the things that you might do in order to make your clients feel welcome and important at your clinic or salon.

Here are some tips that will help your clients feel comfortable.

- Greet them by name and shake hands.
- Smile and make eye contact.
- Sit facing your client, with no barriers in between and at the same height, at a distance where you can speak comfortably.
- Lean forward slightly when talking to them.
- Don't take telephone calls during a consultation or treatment.

YOUR CLIENT'S BODY LANGUAGE

Learning to read your client's body language is a valuable skill in a complementary therapist. Just as you are expressing things through your body language, your client's actions often speak louder than their words. Watch how they are responding to you.

Spotting the signs

If a client feels uncomfortable during a therapy session, how might their body language indicate that to you?

Without saying a word, clients may tell you they are uncomfortable by fidgeting, frowning, wincing, clasping their hands or gripping the treatment table.

Learn to be aware particularly of clients' reactions to pain, etc., and not to be lost in your own thoughts. Clients may not want to let you know they are in pain and may try to hide the fact.

'The last time I had my eyelashes tinted, there was a very painful burning sensation. It usually stings a bit, but this was really uncomfortable and I couldn't stop blinking my eyes. I didn't like to say anything until I realised that it might be a danger signal and I didn't want to risk my eyesight for the sake of appearing brave to the beauty therapist! In the event, there was nothing to worry about, but I was

> **Did you know...?**
>
> When a client goes to visit a professional in their office, clinic or salon, the professional has a great deal of power over how the client feels. This starts the moment a client arrives. You have probably had the experience of being kept waiting by a receptionist 'busy' on a long personal call or too engrossed in a book or magazine to notice you.

> **Did you know...?**
>
> 'Non-verbal communication' is another term for body language.

glad I had said something as you hear horror stories of people being burned and ending up with scars…'

Genevieve, beauty therapy client

If you notice that a client feels uncomfortable or ill at ease during a consultation or session, don't just plough on regardless. It is better to ask them gently whether anything is making them uncomfortable. Their answer may give you valuable feedback on how to proceed with your treatment or how to improve your technique.

Many therapists are embarrassed if a client starts to cry in a session, and feel that they have 'upset' the person and should move on. It is better to say something that affirms the client, such as 'I can see that you feel sad – do you want to say more?', and be guided by them on how to respond. Tears can be very healing, and show that your client has a great deal of trust in you. If the client is upset for long periods of time, they may benefit from a referral to another professional, such as a psychotherapist.

Similarly, sometimes clients feel so relaxed during a treatment that they fall asleep. Many therapists are perfectly comfortable with this, viewing it as a positive benefit. Other therapists seem to find it irritating. This is not likely to help clients relax and enjoy their treatment – if you find yourself becoming annoyed when clients fall asleep, you may like to ask yourself why …

END POINTS

- People often communicate more through their body language than they do by their words.

- Learn how to create a positive and welcoming atmosphere for your clients.

- Use positive body language to show your clients that you are interested in them and are giving them your full attention.

- Be sensitive to what your clients are telling you with their body language.

- Be prepared for clients' need to express some emotions during a consultation.

- Be sure you know when to refer a client for psychotherapy. This is covered in more depth in Section 2, Topic 10.

Topic 14 Communicating with clients (4): receiving negative feedback

Everyone likes being told good things about themselves. As a complementary therapist, you are likely to receive a lot of praise from clients during your time in practice – a good therapist can make a big difference to people's lives and they often want to share that with you.

There may be times, though, when clients have less welcome things to tell you – that they aren't happy with the service you have provided, or feel disappointed or let down. They may have reasonable cause for complaint or you may feel that their comments are unreasonable; whichever is the case, you have to learn to deal with negative feedback in a professional way. This topic looks at this delicate subject.

THE VALUE OF CRITICISM

'Of all the things I have done in my job over the years, I am the most proud of the complaints system we have introduced here. I get a real buzz whenever we get feedback from a patient or a patient's family. It shows that the patients have got the message that serving them is our central concern, and that what happens to them here matters to us.'

Esther Oosthuizen, Head of Public Relations, Baragwanath Hospital, South Africa's largest hospital.

Nobody likes criticism. When it comes, it is all too easy to react defensively. The big challenge is to avoid this knee-jerk reaction. But can it be possible to get to a position, like the Head of PR quoted above, where we can welcome and even encourage feedback from clients? The answer is a resounding 'yes' – and the secret lies in developing a professional attitude.

There are several techniques that can greatly increase your skill in receiving negative feedback from clients.

Your attitude as a person	Your attitude as a professional
'I don't like it when people criticise me.'	'As a professional, I welcome feedback from my clients.'
'I hate it when people are angry with me.'	'In my professional role, I can distance myself temporarily from my personal feelings.'
'I feel small when I think that what I did wasn't good enough.'	'As a professional, I pride myself on providing an excellent service, and welcome every opportunity to improve it even more.'

GET 'INTO ROLE' AS A PROFESSIONAL

Recognise that there is a difference between you as a person and your role as a professional. You can make a huge difference by consciously remaining in your professional role, almost as if you were an actor, and keeping 'in role' when you receive feedback from clients. The chart below gives you some examples.

Feeding back

The next time you receive a service from someone, think about what you would say if you were to give them feedback. You may actually decide to give it to them for real. Start by thinking of some positive feedback, and then follow up with any negative feedback you have about the service they have offered.

The more used you are to giving feedback, the more comfortable you will be with receiving it from your clients. It helps you to get used to the idea that giving and receiving feedback is a normal part of professional life.

RESPOND APPROPRIATELY – 'PRACTISE YOUR LINES'

The first time a client offers you some negative feedback, you may not know what to say, or just be able to manage a rather weak, 'Oh!' There are, however, some standard responses you can make when faced with criticism. This is not to fob off the client – that is not good service – but to keep communication going and to keep it professional.

To start off with, it is a good idea to thank the client – strange as it might seem! For example, you might say: 'Well, thank you for that feedback.' It reminds you that the client is offering you feedback, *not* launching a full-scale assault on your professional integrity.

Some other useful first phrases include:

1 'Thank you for letting me know.'
2 'I didn't realise. I will see that it doesn't happen again.'
3 'I'm very sorry. Can you tell me exactly what happened?'

Example of client feedback		'First response' number...
a)	'Since I had my hair highlighted in your salon last week, my scalp has broken out in blisters.'	
b)	'The toilet paper has run out in the ladies loo.'	
c)	'This is the second time I have booked in for a colour treatment, only to find that you have run out of my usual shade.'	

The correct response

Try matching the 'responses' above to the following examples of feedback from the clients at a hairdressing salon.

You will have noticed that the situations quoted need different responses.

- Scenario (a) is potentially dangerous, involving health and safety issues. You will want to let the client know that you understand the seriousness of the situation, so a response such as (3) is a good start.
- Scenario (b) is probably the least serious – a situation where a simple response like (1) is appropriate.

- Scenario (c) is potentially damaging to your business and you should acknowledge the inconvenience that has been caused to your client, so a response such as (2) is appropriate.

By making an appropriate first response to a client's feedback, you are telling them right away that you are listening to them and will take their comments seriously.

USE POSITIVE BODY LANGUAGE TO ENCOURAGE THE CLIENT

If the feedback is about a potentially serious situation, you will need to find out everything you can about what happened and why.

When inviting feedback from a client, give them your full attention, invite them to sit down, and turn towards them. If the client feels that their experience is important to you, it will make it easier to diffuse a difficult situation and find a positive solution.

During the conversation it is important to listen carefully. In particular:

- don't interrupt
- don't argue
- don't automatically deny everything – they may have a genuine grievance.

Instead, allow the client to tell their story fully. If necessary, ask questions to encourage them to tell you everything. Once they have done this, they will be able to 'hear' your apology, if one is appropriate, and you can find a good solution together.

You can ask a client for a suggestion, or you could offer some alternatives, for example:

- a free colour treatment (for the client in scenario 2 above)

- referral to another therapist
- a promise to change your working practice.

If you promise a client that you will take action in response to their complaint, it is important that you keep your promise.

END POINTS

- Giving and receiving feedback is an everyday part of life for a practising professional.
- Remain professional when receiving negative feedback – don't take it as a personal attack.
- When a client offers feedback, acknowledge what they have said, and invite them to say more.
- Use positive body language to show you are listening.
- When a client has had a chance to tell their story and express their feelings, you will both be in a good position to find a positive solution to the problem.
- Remember that you want to offer an excellent service – anything that will help you improve the service you offer should be regarded positively.

A lot depends on your first consultation with a client. As well as collecting a great deal of information, you will be starting to build your relationship with your client. It is worth planning and preparing for this first contact. This topic looks at the kinds of preparations you can make.

PREPARING FOR THE FIRST CONTACT

Some of the preparations you make will be of a practical nature, to do with how you prepare yourself and surroundings. In Section 2, Topic 1, you will find checklists to help you think about:

- your own appearance
- your practice room or premises, including the supplies you will need.

In order to give your client your full attention, you will need to make sure that you are not tired or hungry or distracted in any way.

It is better not to rush from appointment to appointment. Arrive in good time for your consultation, and give yourself enough time to relax before meeting your client.

BEFORE YOU START...

Your first time
Take a moment to remember the first time you consulted, for instance, a massage therapist, aromatherapist or sports therapist. What were you conscious of feeling?

When about to embark on a new experience or meet a new person, most people feel:

- fearful
- hopeful
- curious.

Some will be more fearful, others more curious – it depends on the person. Clients suffering from a painful or serious condition are more likely to be anxious than those who want, say, a relaxing massage. It helps, if you can, to get the client's feelings out into the open. This is covered in more depth in 'Managing expectations' in the next topic.

FIRST IMPRESSIONS

'Everything the therapist does communicates a message to the client and can affect the treatment. First impressions are very important...'

Louise Tucker,
'An Introductory Guide to Massage'

The first consultation is when you lay the groundwork for a professional and trusting relationship. It is important that you give out the right signals to your client.

Your manner, the way you greet the client, your body language – will all be part of the client's first impression.

What are friends for?
Ask a friend to tell you, honestly, about any mannerisms or habits that you have. Might any of these things be off-putting for your clients?

Topic 13 looks at body language and how you can use it to reassure your client or put them at ease.

WHERE DO I START?

When you first meet a new client, begin by greeting them, perhaps shaking their hand, and inviting them to sit down. You should then introduce yourself, presenting your client with a copy of your business card for future reference.

Don't feel that you have to launch immediately into taking their history. Your main aim at the beginning of the first consultation will be to reassure your client, and make them feel welcome. It is polite to ask whether they are comfortable – whether the room is warm enough for them, or whether they need a glass of water.

You will then be ready to start the consultation proper.

The following checklist will help you plan the time you have with your client, and may be useful as a reminder in the consultation itself.

Some therapists prepare a 'Practice information sheet' to give to clients, to help them remember information about the therapy, practice policies, etc. The next time you are in a salon or clinic, ask for samples of these (see also the Appendix).

Did you know…?

Exchanging a few pleasantries can help clients relax before you 'get down to business'. Most clients will appreciate it if you take a few moments at the start of the consultation to ask about their journey or check that they had no problems finding you.

Checklist: Points to cover in a first consultation

Take a health history from your client, and fill in a record card (see Section 1, Topic 13).	
Find out what the client wants from this consultation with you.	
Find out whether there are any contraindications to the treatment you propose.	
Discuss the client's expectations, and what you can offer.	
Make sure that your client understands that you will keep confidentiality (and explain what this means).	
Make sure the client knows what to expect in the period following the first treatment (reactions to the treatment, possible side effects, and so on).	
Make arrangements, if appropriate, for future meetings.	
Let the client know how to contact you between appointments, if necessary.	
Collect your fee for the consultation.	
Gain the patient's consent to treatment, preferably in the form of a signature.	

Preparing your own leaflet
What would you want to include from the checklist above in your own leaflet? Is there anything that you might want to include that is not in the checklist?

Some therapists like to include on their practice information sheet:

• brief information about the therapy and its history or background

• something about themselves – for

example where they trained, plus a list of their qualifications

- information about how to book sessions and policy about cancellations

- a map or directions to the clinic or salon.

It can be helpful to new clients who have booked over the phone to be sent a sheet with all general information about the clinic or salon, as well as specific information about the treatment they will be receiving, before coming to their first appointment.

END POINTS

- There is a lot to do in your first consultation with a client. Planning pays!

- The first consultation is important in developing a good rapport with your client.

- Many clients are anxious at the start of their first consultation. Take time to make them feel welcome and reassured.

- Your manner, the way you greet the client, your body language – all these will be part of the first impression the client forms of you.

Topic 16 Working with clients (2): managing expectations

When clients arrange an appointment with a therapist, they will have an idea of what the therapy will do for them: in other words, they have expectations. If you meet these expectations, the therapy will be a success and the client will be satisfied. If you don't meet them, the result will be a disappointed client and perhaps no further business. This topic looks at the important issues of working out what clients' expectations of you are, and how to keep those expectations realistic.

WHAT DID YOU EXPECT?

As you saw in Topic 15, most clients arrive for their first consultation with a mixture of feelings including fear, hopefulness and curiosity. As you take the client's history, you may become more aware of the expectations they bring with them.

It is good practice to ask your client what they are hoping for from the consultation with you. If you are clear about their expectations, it is much easier to gear the consultation to their needs.

'WELL, UM...'

It's personal
Think of the health problems suffered by people in your immediate family. Which of these would you find most difficult to talk about, and why?

There are many reasons why clients may find their needs difficult to discuss.

- They may be shy and unused to talking about themselves.
- They may be struggling with a difficult issue in their lives, such as grief or loss, and need you to provide an encouraging environment in which to talk.
- They may feel that their hopes and feelings are unreasonable.

- They may be unused to exposing their body to a stranger.
- They may feel embarrassed. Among the things that clients might find it difficult to discuss are areas such as: weight loss, sexual problems, hair loss, fertility problems, bowel/continence problems, menopause, sexually transmitted diseases, drug and alcohol abuse problems and mental illness.

Many practitioners find it useful to have a standard client record form that deals with each area of the body in turn. They use this to establish clients' state of health and to find out what they want from their treatment.

It isn't always easy to find out what clients' expectations are. They themselves may not be fully aware of what they want from their session with you.

Matching up to expectations
Read the list of client statements in the left-hand column in the table on the next page. Then try to match each one with a statement in the right-hand column that describes how that client might be feeling inside:

Did **you know...?**

Many parts of the human body are no-go areas in day-to-day discussions. People may never have needed to use words like 'vagina' or 'testicles', and so feel shy about saying them.

Client says:	Client feels:
a) 'I don't think it's that much of a problem, but my husband persuaded me to come to see you.'	1 Client may be fearful that they will never get relief from their symptoms, or angry at having been ignored by other professionals
b) 'I've already seen a massage therapist, but he just made it worse.'	2 Client may not want treatment from you at all – may only be there to keep her husband happy!
c) 'I told the doctor, but he said there was nothing he could do'	3 Client may be sceptical about whether *you* can help

One way of matching the statement to the feelings is (a) – 2; (b) – 3; (c) – 1.

USING A TREATMENT PLAN

Before starting the treatment of a client, many practitioners like to agree a 'treatment plan' with them. This helps to avoid unrealistic expectations and disappointed hopes.

A treatment plan is based on:

- the client's health history (including any contraindications), based on the record card you have written up
- what the client wants from the consultation (both the things they have told you, and anything you 'pick up' from what they say)
- your own assessment of what you can and can't do for the client.

GOOD NEWS/BAD NEWS

If you feel that the client has expectations that you cannot meet, you need to make this clear as soon as possible.

Bad news
Think back to a situation where you had to disappoint someone because you were not able to do what they wanted. How did you break the news to them?

One way of giving a person disappointing news, is to use a variation on the good news/bad news technique.

You can do this in stages. The checklist below may help you to structure the delivery of any disappointing news you have to give to a client.

END POINTS

- Managing your clients' expectations is an important skill to develop.

- Particular care is needed in situations where clients:

  - are shy about discussing with you what they want from treatment

  - have a serious illness and/or unreasonable hopes

  - are bringing emotional baggage with them.

- A treatment plan, agreed with your client, can help avoid a situation in which your client is disappointed.

- A professional therapist will always:

  - be clear about what they can offer to clients and what they can't

  - will always offer the client an alternative, where one exists.

Did **you know...?**

For some clients, complementary therapy is a 'last resort'. One of the most difficult situations of all for a therapist is when a client has a serious or potentially life-threatening illness, and has secret (or spoken) hopes that you will be able to cure them.

Checklist: Good news/bad news

Step	Example of what you might say:
Affirm the client's feelings.	'I understand that the pain in your joints from arthritis is getting increasingly hard for you to bear.'
Let them know that you understand what they want.	'I know that you are hoping that reflexology will help relieve or even stop the pain.'
Tell them, tactfully, what you cannot do ('bad news').	'I am afraid that the primary goal of reflexology is not pain relief and so I can't promise you that.'
Tell them what you can do ('good news').	'However, many people with arthritis do get great benefits from reflexology. If you decide to go ahead, you should find it has benefits in terms of relaxation, etc…'
Offer them a choice.	'I can offer you the choice of carrying on with the session or, if you prefer, you can go away and mull it over. I won't charge you for this session if you decide you don't want reflexology.'

Did you know…?

A good way of getting feedback from your clients is to ask them at the beginning of each consultation how the last one was for them.

Section 3

The environment

Topic 1 Legislation and regulation: health and safety at work

This topic looks at one of the most important areas of legislation for people running your kind of business – health and safety at work. This legislation requires you to make sure your premises are safe for yourself, anyone who works for you, and your clients.

'I was really worried about all the legislation and regulations when I was thinking of starting up on my own. But I talked to a friend who already has her own beauty therapy clinic in another town and she gave me some really helpful advice. I had a look on the Internet as well. Most of it is common sense really but you need to know exactly what the law says so that you can make sure you are doing the right thing.'

Susan, beauty therapist

Other topics in this section cover important aspects of working safely: first aid; fire safety; infections and hygiene; sterilisation and waste disposal.

LAWS AND REGULATIONS

There is one main law on health and safety at work:

- Health and Safety at Work Act 1974.

There are also many regulations. Some of the most important are:

- The Management of Health and Safety at Work Regulations 1992
- The Workplace (Health, Safety and Welfare) Regulations 1992
- The Provision and Use of Work Equipment Regulations 1992.

Together, these mean that before you start running a business you have to look carefully at the working environment to make sure you will not be putting anyone at risk. This is called making a risk assessment. Start thinking about this next.

Look at the checklist on the following page. This is a long and fairly daunting list, but you need to be able to answer 'yes' to all these questions before you go into business. It is illegal to operate a business unless you know you meet the requirements of the Health and Safety at Work Act (HASWA) and the regulations.

If you answered 'No' or 'Not sure' to any of these questions, you need some advice or more information. You can get this from the Health and Safety Executive (HSE).

LIFTING AND CARRYING

It may be especially important in healthcare and therapy work to know how to lift and carry things. The Manual Handling Operations Regulations 1992 cover:

- lifting
- lowering
- pushing
- pulling
- carrying
- moving.

These regulations may apply if you handle stock, move equipment or lift clients, and

Did **you know...?**

On-the-job supplies of drugs and alcohol account for 15 to 30 per cent of all accidents at work.

Did **you know...?**

If you employ other people, you must either display the Health and Safety Law poster or hand out a Health and Safety Law leaflet, both available from the HSE.

Checklist: Health and safety arrangements

Do you know…?	Yes/No/ Not sure
how to handle equipment and materials safely	
how to transport and store substances such as dyes, oils, creams	
what equipment you need to provide to keep your workplace safe	
how to keep entrance and exit points safe	
what facilities you need to provide to keep your premises safe for anyone who uses them	
what ventilation, temperature control and lighting you need to keep your premises safe and healthy	
how you will keep your premises clean	
how you will dispose of any waste	
whether your washing and toilet facilities are adequate	
whether your drinking water supply is adequate	
how you will store your work clothes	
whether your premises are big enough for health and safety requirements	
whether you have the right kind of rest and eating facilities	
whether the type of glazing in your windows meets health and safety requirements	
whether you have suitable floor coverings	
whether your furniture is in good order and meets health and safety requirements (you must provide each employee with a chair)	
whether stairs and corridors are free from obstructions	
if you have employees, which member of staff will be your health and safety representative	
what health and safety information you need to give any employees	
if you have any equipment, whether staff are trained to use it safely	
whether maintenance records for equipment are up to date	
what other training and supervision any employees need to maintain health and safety	

can certainly help reduce the risk of back or other injuries. You may also like to talk to a good physiotherapist who could show you the best ways of lifting.

HAZARDOUS SUBSTANCES AND MATERIALS

If you are working with chemicals or any other potentially dangerous materials, you will need to know how to use them safely and train any staff in using them safely too. This is covered by The Control of Substances Hazardous to Health Regulations 1992 (COSHH).

You may need to wear protective equipment such as gloves or a mask. You will also have to supply these for anyone who works for you. The Personal Protective Equipment at Work Regulations 1992 cover this aspect of health and safety.

THE HEALTH AND SAFETY EXECUTIVE

The role of the Health and Safety Executive (HSE) is to ensure that risks to people's health and safety from work activities are properly controlled. The HSE is overseen by the Health and Safety Commission (HSC).

Your local HSE office can send an inspector to your premises to check that you are meeting the standards required.

There are many other regulations that cover health and safety at work. If you want more information on these or any other health and safety issues, you can contact your local HSE office (find the number in the phone book under Health and Safety). They also have a number of helpful publications (see the list in Section 5).

'I was a bit nervous about contacting my local HSE in case they sent someone round to "inspect" me. But the person there was really helpful and sorted out the queries I had about what I had to do and what I didn't have to do.'

Bryan, masseur

END POINTS

- By law, you have to make sure your premises are safe for yourself, anyone working for you, and your clients.

- The main law on health and safety at work is the Health and Safety at Work Act 1974.

- Other regulations cover particular aspects of work, such as using equipment, lifting and carrying, and handling hazardous substances.

- If you want more information on health and safety issues, you can contact your local HSE office.

Did **you know…?**

If you employ five people or more, you have to write a health and safety policy statement, and display it so that the people working for you can see it.

If you employ ten or more employees, you also have to keep an accident book.

This topic looks at employment legislation – laws that govern how you look after your employees. If you don't employ anyone else you probably don't need to read this now, unless you are planning to take any exams. If you do start employing other people, it will be helpful to read through this topic first.

DECIDING TO TAKE ON STAFF

If you want to expand your business, you will almost certainly have to take on staff. There are several other topics in this book that look at these areas.

- Section 1, Topic 12 is about recruiting and retaining staff, and maintaining a good working relationship with them.
- The health and safety of employees is covered in Section 3, Topic 1.
- Employees' tax and national insurance is covered in Section 1, Topic 5.
- Employers' liability insurance is covered in Section 1, Topic 11.
- Discrimination is covered in Section 3, Topic 3.

In this topic we will be focusing on the main laws and regulations that govern employment.

Checklist: Employment rights

	Tick here
Employees must have a written statement of their employment details, including details of pay, terms and conditions of employment, pension rights and disciplinary procedures.	
Employees must have a written, itemised pay statement.	
Both employees and employers must have a minimum period of notice – this depends on the length of service.	
If employees are dismissed, they must have a written statement giving reasons for the dismissal.	
Employees must not be unfairly dismissed.	
Employees are entitled to appeal to an industrial tribunal if they feel they have been unfairly dismissed.	
Employees must receive redundancy payments if they:	
• are between 16 and 65 years old	
• have worked for their employer for a continuous period of 104 weeks	
• are insurable for all benefits under the Social Welfare Acts	
• normally work 18 hours or more per week.	

EMPLOYEES' RIGHTS

Employees' rights are covered by the 1996 Employment Rights Act. This brought UK law into line with European law. The main rights are listed on the previous page. Tick the box on the right-hand side if you are confident that you can meet the standards required by law.

If you were not sure about any of these employees' rights, you need to get some advice and information before you go any further – see page 129.

WORKING TIME REGULATIONS 1998

The Working Time Regulations 1998 (often referred to as WTR) provide additional rights for employees.

- Employees need work no more than an average of 48 hours a week – but can work more hours if they choose to.

- Night workers need work no more than eight hours in every 24 hours, and they have the right to free health assessments.

- All workers have the right to 11 hours rest each day, and to one day off each week.

- All workers have the right to take an in-work rest break, if the working day is longer than six hours.

- All workers have the right to four weeks' paid leave each year.

WRITING A CONTRACT OF EMPLOYMENT

As an employer, you must give each person you employ a contract of employment setting out the terms of employment, within two months of their start date. Both parties should sign the main copy of the contract, and this should be kept somewhere secure, such as in a locked filing cabinet. Each employee should be given their own copy to keep.

If you want to draw up a contract for the first time, go through the points in the checklist on page 128, filling in the details for one of your employees. You should then have a basis for a contract, which you can adapt for other employees. If possible, use a word processor to make it easier to adapt the basic contract for each employee.

You may also wish to include a statement about training. It is common for the employee to be asked to pay back a proportion of training costs if they leave your employment: normally, if the person leaves within three months, they would pay back 90% of the training costs; if they leave within six months, they would repay 50% of the costs, and so on. There is a sample contract of employment in Section 5.

SICKNESS AND MATERNITY BENEFIT

If you employ staff, you are liable to pay Statutory Sick Pay (SSP) to an employee who is off work for more than four days in a row. You will need to decide how you want your employees to notify you of their illness; many employers ask for a doctor's certificate.

Statutory Maternity Pay (SMP) is the maternity benefit paid out by employers to employees and is payable for up to 26 weeks from the eleventh week before the baby is expected, provided:

- the employee has been in continuous employment for at least 26 weeks preceding the 15th week before the expected week of childbirth

- she earns at least the lower earnings limit for National Insurance contributions (£79 per week, as of April 2004); and

Checklist: Contract of employment

Tick each point as you complete it. If you need any help or information, see the references section at the end of this book.	Tick when complete
Your name	
Name of employee	
Employee's job title (attach job description)	
Place of work	
Date employee started work	
Hours of work	
Holiday entitlement including public holidays (be careful when working out part-time holiday entitlement)	
Salary (and salary scale if there is one)	
Any commission structure (e.g. on sale of products)	
Payment dates and method	
Sickness and injury arrangements including entitlement to sick pay	
Grievance procedures	
Pension scheme (if any)	
Period of notice for either party	
Disciplinary procedures	

• she has given due statutory notice to her employer, or whoever is responsible for the payment of the statutory maternity benefit.

The employee must inform you of her intention to stop working at least three weeks before she intends to do so. She must produce her maternity certificate within three weeks of starting her maternity pay period.

DISMISSAL

If you are thinking of dismissing an employee, you need to know what you are doing. If you unfairly dismiss someone, they can take you to an industrial tribunal and claim compensation. The legislation is

there to protect people from being dismissed for no good reason.

Generally speaking, you can dismiss people for:

• incompetence

• misconduct

• redundancy

• special circumstances (e.g. loss of driving licence if driving is an essential part of the job)

• any other significant business reason.

If employees are dismissed, you must give them a written statement giving reasons for their dismissal, and they must not be unfairly dismissed. Examples of unfair dismissal include:

- dismissal without following the correct procedures

- dismissal without giving the employee verbal and written warnings

- dismissal because an employee has taken part in union activities or industrial action.

Instant dismissal for a major offence, such as theft, is legal.

GETTING HELP

Employment law is complex and constantly changing. If you are a first-time employer, you can get help and advice from your local Employment Service (in the Phone Book under 'Employment').

ACAS has a network of telephone helplines giving free help and information to anyone with a work problem, including information about employees' rights – see the ACAS website for regional telephone numbers.

Stressline offers a 24-hour helpline and support service for the workplace, including counselling and training.

Employers/Employees Helpline is a government initiative offering help and advice for employers and self-employed people concerning tax, National Insurance and VAT, as well as benefits such as SSP and SMP.

Please see the Resources section for contact details for these and other useful references.

END POINTS

- Employing staff carries certain legal responsibilities.

- Employment law changes rapidly and it is important to keep up to date.

- You must provide a contract of employment specifying certain aspects of the job including:

  – brief description of the job

  – hours of work

  – salary and commission

  – holiday entitlement

  – period of notice

  – disciplinary procedure.

- You must have a good reason if you dismiss someone, and you must follow the correct procedures.

> Did **you know...?**
>
> 11,565 unfair dismissals cases went to industrial tribunals in 2000/01 and 48.5% were upheld.

Topic 3 Legislation and regulation: data protection and equal opportunities

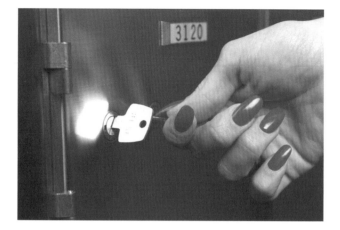

This topic looks at two important aspects of the law:

- **data protection** – making sure any data you have on clients or employees is secure
- **equal opportunities** – making sure you do not discriminate against employees or clients.

There is more on keeping records in Section 1, Topic 13 and on employment legislation in Section 3, Topic 2.

Checklist: Complying with the Data Protection Act

Find out whether your business meets the data protection requirements. Tick the boxes on the right-hand side if you think you meet these data protection requirements. If you aren't sure, contact the Information Commissioner's Office for advice (details in Section 5).

Is your data…?	
fairly and lawfully processed – this usually means getting the person's consent before you store the information, and observing confidentiality	
limited to the information you need – in other words, stick to the data you need; don't collect information on anything else	
only used in ways that are compatible with the reasons for which you collected the data – so if you collect information for treatment purposes, you must not pass that information on to other companies, or use it for a mailshot	
only kept for as long as it is needed	
secure – kept somewhere safe, e.g. a locked filing cabinet or room, or if computerised, with a password	

DATA PROTECTION

In order to treat clients, you will need to collect personal information from them. If you have employees, you will also keep information about them on file. The collection and storage of any information (or 'data') like this is tightly controlled by the Data Protection Act 1998. This law covers all records, whether they are stored manually or on a computer.

If you have employees, they have the right to know what personal data you hold and

should be given an opportunity to check that it is correct. Many employers do this by giving employees a printout of the information on file, perhaps once a year, and asking them to check and sign it.

Data Protection Registrar

If you keep information on a computer about your clients, employees or anyone else, you may need to register with the Data Protection Registrar. You can register by filling in a notification form which you can download from the Data Protection website (www.dataprotection.gov.uk). You can also register online or by contacting the Notification helpline on 01625 545 740.

Failure to register if you need to is a criminal offence, so it's worth checking this. If you are not sure, phone the Notification helpline. You can also register voluntarily if you only hold manual records.

EQUAL OPPORTUNITIES

If you employ people, you will need to be aware of three main pieces of legislation:

- The Sex Discrimination Act 1975 – makes it illegal for employers to discriminate between men and women
- The Race Relations Act 1976 – makes it illegal for employers to discriminate against anyone on the grounds of race
- The Equal Pay Act 1976 – gives men and women the right to equal pay and benefits.

There is an example of a job advertisement, which contains an equal opportunities statement, in Section 5.

Checklist: Equal opportunities

If you employ staff, check out whether your business is providing equal opportunities.

	Yes	Not sure	No
Do you make it clear in your recruitment advertising that you are an equal opportunities employer? (For example, you can say 'We are an equal opportunities employer' at the bottom of the advert.)			
When you are interviewing new staff, do you ask questions that do not discriminate? (For example, do you ask all candidates about whether they can operate equipment, not just female candidates?)			
Do you give all staff equal opportunities for promotion?			
Do you pay female staff equal pay for doing the same or broadly similar work as male staff?			
Are the benefits for female staff equal to those for male staff?			

If you answered 'Yes' to all the questions, you are probably doing well on equal opportunities, although you will need to keep yourself up to date as the legislation often changes. If you answered 'No' or 'Not sure', you may need to contact The Equal Opportunities Commission or the Commission for Racial Equality for more information.

There are also several useful publications on equal opportunities – see page 205.

THE DISABILITY DISCRIMINATION ACT 1995

The Disability Discrimination Act 1995 means that it is illegal to treat a person less favourably because of their disability. The law was phased in gradually, with the final phase, making 'reasonable adjustments' to premises, coming into force in October 2004.

The law applies not only to employers but also to 'service providers' – that's you. This

Did **you know…?**

Sex and race discrimination applications represented 17% of all applications received by the Employment Tribunal Office in 2001.

131

means that if any of your clients have a disability, you have to ensure that they have equal access to your services. This might involve practical changes, such as placing a wheelchair ramp over a step. But it might also involve changing the way you think about disabled people, perhaps arranging for you and your staff to have training in disability awareness.

In any profession concerned with body image and self-improvement (including complementary, beauty and sports therapies), it is especially important to ensure that disabled people feel that they have equal access and rights.

If you are not sure about any aspect of disability law or you want more information about disability discrimination, contact the Disability Rights Commission (DRC) – contact details in Section 5.

Checklist: Providing equal access

	Yes	Not sure	No
Do you welcome disabled clients to your service?			
Have you made sure that there are no physical barriers to disabled clients using your service, e.g. stairs, ban on dogs (some people have a guide dog), treatment room difficult for people with mobility problems?			
Are you and your staff trained in disability awareness?			
Do you have a procedure at work to challenge immediately any comments about someone's disability?			
Do you make disabled clients feel that their treatment is just as important to you as the treatment of other clients?			

END POINTS

- If you collect and store information about clients or employees, you must comply with the Data Protection Act 1998.

- Employees have the right to know what personal data you hold and should have an opportunity to check that it is correct.

- If you keep information on a computer about your clients, employees or anyone else, you may need to register with the Data Protection Registrar.

- If you employ other people, you will need to be aware of legislation regarding sex discrimination, race discrimination and equal pay.

- Under the Disability Discrimination Act 1995, it is illegal to treat a person less favourably because of their disability.

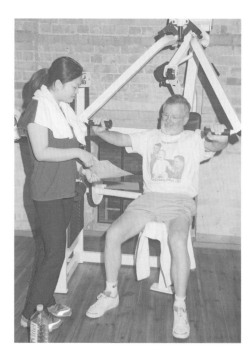

Topic 4 Legislation and regulation: professional membership and licensing

Most areas of complementary and healthcare therapy have a professional body that acts as a central source of information, help and support. This topic looks at the benefits of joining a professional organisation. It also looks at the question of whether you need to have a licence to operate.

JOINING A PROFESSIONAL ORGANISATION

If you are starting up in business, it's a very good idea to join a professional organisation. Some of the many reasons why are listed here:

- certificate of membership
- legal advice
- helpline and other advice services
- insurance cover
- discounts on products, equipment and courses
- credit card (subject to status)
- advertising
- continuing professional development opportunities – seminars, conferences, workshops, refresher courses
- publications – sometimes a regular magazine, newsletter or journal
- network/forum to contact other members
- use of organisation's logo in advertising
- representation on professional issues in the media.

'I have used the helpline of my professional organisation several times. Last time I had a specific question about whether to use a certain treatment on a client with Parkinson's disease. It's good to know that there's someone on the other end of the line who understands what you are doing and is there to help when you need it.'

Wanda, aromatherapist

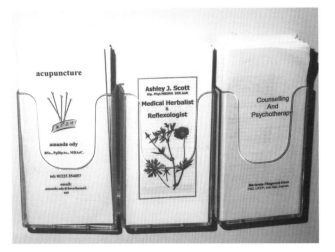

There are many professional organisations for people working in therapy and healthcare. Some of them are listed on the next page. Tick the ones you would like to know more about.

A list of professional organisations for complementary and alternative therapies, including sports therapy, is available on www.internethealthlibrary.com/Prime-pages/A-ZDirProfAssoc.htm

See also:
www.fimed.org
www.nhsalliance.org
www.bodymind.co.uk

Many professional organisations also have codes of conduct or codes of ethics that members are bound by. In this way, belonging to an organisation can give clients confidence in the services you provide. There is more on this in Section 2, Topic 5.

'It would have been a nightmare trying to organise all my own insurance. My professional body has a tailor-made insurance package for beauty therapists.'

Debbie, beauty therapist

Would like to meet...

Name of organisation	Website	Tick if interested
Aromatherapy Organisations Council (AOC)	www.aoc.uk.net	
Association of Reflexologists (AOR)	www.aor.org.uk	
British Association for Counselling and Psychotherapy (BACP)	www.bac.co.uk	
British Association of Beauty Therapists and Cosmetologists (BABTAC)	www.babtac.com	
British Association of Occupational Therapists (BAOT)	www.cot.org.uk	
British Complementary Medicine Association (BCMA)	www.bcma.co.uk	
British Reflexology Association (BRA)	www.britreflex.co.uk	
Chartered Society of Physiotherapy (CSP)	www.csp.org.uk	
Federation of Holistic Therapists (FHT)	www.fht.org.uk	
International Guild of Professional Practitioners	www.igpp.co.uk	
Guild of Professional Beauty Therapists	www.beautyserve.com	
Independent Professional Therapists International (IPTI)	www.iptiuk.com	
Institute for/British General Council of Complementary Medicine (ICM/BGCCM)	www.icmedicine.co.uk	
International Federation of Aromatherapists (IFA)	www.int-fed.aromatherapy.co.uk	
Institute of Sports Massage & Physical Therapy	www.ismpt.ire	
The London & Counties Society of Physiologists	www.lcsp.uk.com	

Please note: inclusion in this list does not represent an endorsement.

'I've been an acupuncturist for 15 years, so I have been very grateful for all the refresher courses my professional organisation runs. It's also a good chance to meet other acupuncturists and compare notes and ideas.'

Pablo, acupuncturist

LICENSING

Some businesses must have a licence to operate. For example, if you are involved in acupuncture, electrolysis or ear piercing, you have to register with your local authority under the Local Government Miscellaneous Act 1982.

The environmental health department will make an inspection. If you are successful, you will be issued with a licence to operate. There is a charge for the licence. Contact your local authority if you think you might need to have a licence.

Residential care home managers

Residential care homes must be registered with the National Care Standards Commission (NCSC), a new public body set up under the Care Standards Act 2000 to regulate social care, and private and voluntary health care services in England. Each care home has to meet National Minimum Standards and the manager is assessed for their 'fitness' to run the home.

To register, contact the NCSC whose address is included in Section 5.

END POINTS

- If you are starting up in business, joining a professional organisation can provide both practical help and moral support.

- Many professional organisations have codes of conduct or codes of ethics that members are bound by.

- Some businesses must have a licence to operate; you should check whether this applies to you.

- A comprehensive list of therapies and their related professional organisations can be found on www.internethealthlibrary.com/Prime-pages/A-ZDirProfAssoc.htm

Topic 5 First aid

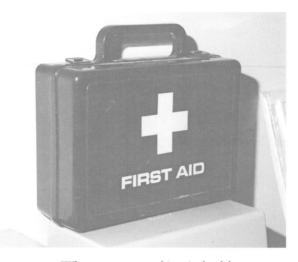

When you are working in healthcare or therapy, it is essential to know how to give first aid. To do this you need to do a recognised first-aid training course from, for example, the British Red Cross, St John Ambulance or St Andrew's Ambulance Association (see page 207, Resources section). This topic looks at having a first-aid box, giving basic first aid, and keeping an accident book.

FIRST-AID MANUAL

This topic doesn't give you a crash course in first aid – that would be impossible in a book of this nature, and downright dangerous. Most beauty and complementary therapists will have to do first-aid training in order to qualify.

Even at a very basic level, putting someone in the recovery position is best done by someone who has had face-to-face training as a first aider – although in a real emergency, that may not be an option; it is better to try to help, rather than let someone choke because they are in the wrong position.

You will find useful information about all aspects of first aid in the *First Aid Manual* (the authorised manual of the British Red Cross, St John Ambulance and St Andrew's Ambulance Association) published by Dorling Kindersley. This is an excellent book, with clear instructions and diagrams. If you don't have a copy, buy one as soon as possible and keep it somewhere handy so that you can refer to it, even after proper first-aid training.

More important, you should think seriously about getting first-aid training yourself, so that you will be ready to take action in case of an accident or emergency. Training is provided by several organisations, including:

- British Red Cross Society
- St John Ambulance
- St Andrew's Ambulance Association.

National addresses are provided in the Resources section, but you will find details of local branches in the phone book.

We strongly urge you to complete a recognised three-day training course.

FIRST-AID BOX

There is no standard list of items to include in a first-aid box. You have to do your own assessment of what is needed. Use the checklist on the following page as a general guide. Remember, these are only suggestions – for more advice, contact the British Red Cross or St John Ambulance.

It's a good idea to keep all the items in a green box with a white cross on it, as this is likely to be recognised as the first-aid box. Put a card in it giving the names and contact details for local doctors and hospitals, etc. Check it regularly and use your own checklist to make sure it is stocked.

You will find more information about first aid materials in the *First-Aid Manual*.

Checklist: Contents of a first aid box

Work through the following checklist and compare it with the contents of your own first-aid box. If you don't have a first-aid box, this checklist could be the start of your shopping list. Make sure you know what each item is for and when you might use it.

In your first-aid box, do you have...?	Yes	Not sure	No
leaflet giving general guidance on first aid			
20 individually wrapped sterile adhesive dressings (plasters – assorted sizes)			
two sterile eye pads			
six medium-sized (approx 12cm x 12cm) individually wrapped sterile unmedicated wound dressings			
two large (approx 18cm x 18cm) sterile individually wrapped unmedicated wound dressings			
four individually wrapped triangular bandages (preferably sterile)			
six safety pins			
one pair of disposable gloves			
sterile water			

> **Did you know...?**
>
> Under the Health and Safety (First-Aid) Regulations 1981, you have to provide adequate facilities to enable first aid to be given to employees.

GIVING BASIC FIRST AID

'A wasp stung a client on her mouth during a consultation. Within seconds her whole mouth had swelled up and she began to panic. I quickly prepared an ice pack and applied it to her mouth. Then I phoned for an ambulance to take her to the local A & E department.'

Pearl, Bach Flower Remedy consultant

It is very important for you to know how to give first aid to a client (or employee) until you can get medical help. However, you must be aware that doing the wrong thing could result in a lawsuit rather than gratitude. Even though, in the case above, the therapist knew that antihistamine would probably help to reduce the swelling, she quite rightly didn't offer any medication. Whatever your instincts, you would be unwise even to offer aspirin or paracetamol, because of the risk of litigation.

Check how well prepared you are for medical emergencies by using the checklist on the following page. Most of these incidents are not serious, but one or two of them could be life-threatening if you don't know what to do.

If you answered 'Yes' to all of them, you have probably done some first-aid training recently. If not, you should do a first-aid training course (see page 136).

'I was working in the salon when there was a terrible screeching of brakes. A car had crashed into a pillar box, after swerving to avoid an elderly woman crossing the road. The driver was unhurt, but shaken, but the woman was in a terrible state. She was a horrible grey colour, sweating and shaking like a leaf. I was sure she was in shock.

We brought her into the salon and called for an ambulance, but no one was quite

Checklist: In case of emergency...

Work through the following checklist noting whether you would know what to do in each case. When you have finished, compare your notes with what is suggested in the First Aid Manual.

Do you know what to do if someone...?	Yes	Not sure	No
faints			
burns or scalds themselves			
has an epileptic fit			
is bleeding			
becomes hysterical			
has a heart attack			
loses consciousness			
has heat exhaustion			
twists their ankle			
has an asthma attack			
goes into a diabetic coma			
has a nose bleed			
is stung by an insect			
is hyperventilating			
has a migraine			
becomes dizzy			
has an electric shock			
has an electrical burn			
has sun burn			

sure what to do next. One client suggested giving her strong sweet tea, another said whisky – I knew both of these were wrong as I'd recently completed a proper first-aid training course. Instead, we laid her down, raised her legs, kept her warm and just moistened her lips with water. One of the other therapists checked the first-aid book, just to make sure there was nothing else we could do. The woman was fine eventually, and the paramedics said I'd done all the right things, which pleased me.'

Debbie, beautician

GETTING MEDICAL HELP

Bear in mind that people may not necessarily be grateful for your intervention. Should anything go wrong, you might find yourself involved in a lawsuit. However, there are some common-sense guidelines you can follow.

- Get help if you are at all uncertain or think the situation merits it, e.g. you think someone needs medical help.

- Err on the side of caution, i.e. if in doubt, ask for help. It's not always easy to know when you should or shouldn't get help. Someone may say 'Oh, I'll be fine', whereas you think they definitely aren't fine.

- **Never** give your own medication – even aspirin – in case the person has an adverse reaction.

- If you don't want to leave someone alone, get someone else to phone. Ask them to come back and confirm that they've made the call and that help is on the way.

- If a trained first aider is available, follow their instructions.

- Dial 999. Emergency phone calls are free and can be made on any telephone, including car phones and portable phones.

- If someone is hurt, ask for the ambulance service; the control officer will pass on messages to other services (e.g. police) if necessary.

- Give information that you are asked for. This will include:
  – your phone number
  – your exact location
  – the type and seriousness of the incident
  – details about the casualty (age, sex, condition).

THE RECOVERY POSITION

If someone is unconscious, there is a safe position to put them in which allows them to breathe easily and stops them choking on any vomit. This is called the **recovery position**.

Face-to-face training is by far the best way of learning how to put someone in the recovery position and you should make it a priority to be trained in first aid.

In the meantime, if someone collapses in your salon or clinic, you may have to put the person in the recovery position. First:

- check their airway is clear
- check they are breathing
- check they have a pulse.

Then lie them on their front, with their head tilted back slightly to keep the airway clear.

WARNING!

If casualty may have head or neck injuries:

- ensure head and neck are supported at all times
- do not allow rotation between head and spine
- do not tilt head back if neck injury is suspected.

Source: www.stjohn.org.au/emergency/ html/recovery.htm

Stay with them reassuring them while someone else rings 999 for an ambulance. If you are on your own, ring quickly and return to the person as soon as you can. Check frequently to make sure the casualty's airway is still open and he or she is still breathing.

KEEPING AN ACCIDENT BOOK

If you have ten or more people working for you, you have to keep a record of any accidents – usually in an accident book. It's a good idea to keep one anyway, even if you employ fewer than ten people, then you have a record of what happened in case there is an insurance claim later on (see Section 1, Topic 11).

A record of an accident should include:

- the date and time of the accident
- the nature of the accident, including where it happened
- a short description of any action taken
- your signature and the signature of the person who had the accident, confirming that the record is accurate.

An example of a page from an accident book is included in Section 5.

THE REPORTING ON INJURIES, DISEASE AND DANGEROUS OCCURRENCES REGULATIONS 1985

The Reporting on Injuries, Disease and Dangerous Occurrences Regulations 1985 (RIDDOR) specify that if an employee or trainee has a personal injury at work resulting in:

- death
- major injury
- more than three days off work
- disease
- dangerous occurrences

it must be reported. You can find more information about RIDDOR at www.riddor.gov.uk or from the Incident Contact Centre, whose address is included in Section 5.

END POINTS

- Get first-aid training! Don't leave it to someone else to take action.
- Keep a well-stocked first-aid kit. Check its contents regularly.
- Keep a copy of the *First-Aid Manual* somewhere handy.
- Be ready to get medical help if necessary. If in doubt, get help.
- The recovery position is a safe position that allows an unconscious person to breathe easily and stops them choking on any vomit.
- If you have ten or more people working for you, you have to keep a record of any accidents.

Topic 6 Fire safety

This topic looks at fire safety and what to do in the event of a fire. It also looks at how to use electrical equipment safely. These are really important issues for anyone running their own business – your safety and the safety of your clients and staff must always come first.

'We work on the ground floor of a tall building so we are very conscious of fire risks. If we had a fire, we would be putting not only ourselves at risk but all the people who work in the floors above us too.'

Andy, sports masseur

FIRE-FIGHTING EQUIPMENT

Your salon should be equipped with the correct fire-fighting equipment. What you will need depends on the type of salon or clinic you have (what equipment you use), how big the salon or clinic is (how many treatment rooms), and how many people use it.

There are different kinds of fire extinguishers for different kinds of fire. We have listed them in the checklist below.

The fire officer will also be able to advise

you about other types of fire safety equipment you may need, e.g. fire blankets. It is a good idea to contact the fire service in any case, as you may need a record of their visit for insurance purposes.

When you have sorted out what you need, make sure that:

• you have it checked annually by a qualified electrician and marked with the date it was checked

Checklist: Types of fire extinguisher

Work through the checklist and tick the fire extinguishers that you think you will need. Then ask your local fire safety officer to give you advice on what equipment you need and where you should put it – contact your local fire service (under 'Fire' in the Phone Book).

Type of extinguisher	Colour of label	What it's used for	Tick here
Water	Whole extinguisher is red	Paper, cloth or wood only	
Foam	Cream or buff	Paper, cloth, wood or liquids, but not chip or fat pan fires	
Carbon dioxide	Black	Dry fires including electrical	
Multi-purpose dry powder	Blue	Dry fires including electrical; liquids, but not chip or fat pan fires	

- it is fixed securely to the wall
- you know how to use it and it is not too heavy for you to use
- any staff know how, and are able, to use it too.

Look in your Yellow Pages for 'fire extinguishing equipment' to find local sources of fire extinguishers and other fire protection equipment.

EVACUATING A BUILDING

Although you might be able to put a small fire out with fire-fighting equipment, a larger fire will mean you have to evacuate the building. This is everybody's nightmare, but being prepared can make all the difference. Work through the following checklist to see how well prepared you are for dealing with a fire.

If you tick 'Yes' for everything, you should have the basis for an evacuation plan. Type it out and pin it on a wall in your salon. If you employ staff, go through it with them so that everyone knows the emergency procedure.

If you tick 'Not sure' or 'No' for anything,

your salon isn't safe – you are not confident that you could get everyone out in the event of a fire. Talk to the fire safety officer about an evacuation plan. If your therapy involves clients removing clothing you should, ideally, make sure clients have time to get dressed before evacuating. If there isn't time, at least try to make sure their modesty is preserved, e.g. by letting them cover up with towels or with a robe – providing they can still get out in time.

THE FIRE PRECAUTIONS ACT 1971

This act says that employers have a duty to provide a fire escape for employees and members of the public. A fire certificate is required if:

- you employ more than 20 people at any time
- there are more than 10 people working anywhere other than the ground floor
- the total number of people working in the building, including the salon, is more than 20.

Checklist: In the event of a fire...

	Yes	Not sure	No
Could you organise people to move swiftly and quietly out of the building while you are contacting the emergency fire services?			
Do you know what the best exit is? (Is it always kept clear? Is it marked 'Fire exit'?)			
Is there an assembly point outside where you could tell everyone to wait?			
Do you know to leave belongings behind?			
Do you know why you shouldn't use a lift in the event of a fire?			
Do you keep a list of each day's clients so that you could check that everyone has got out?			

The fire certificate states:

- the maximum number of people who can safely be employed on the premises at any one time
- what the means of escape are
- that exits must be marked as fire escapes
- any special risks.

If you share your building with other businesses, you need to be sure there is a valid fire certificate. If you are in any doubt as to how you stand with regards to a fire certificate, contact your Local Fire Authority and they will be more than happy to help.

KEEPING ELECTRICAL EQUIPMENT SAFE

'We use electrical equipment all the time, so we have to be very careful about storing and maintaining it. We check once a month for frayed cables and loose plugs and have the equipment serviced once a year.'

Pirrin, physiotherapist

In healthcare and beauty therapy, you will almost certainly be using electrical equipment. This may just be a computer for your accounts, or it may be equipment for the therapy you provide, e.g. for massage, electrolysis or ultrasound. Whatever equipment you use, it is very important to install, use, store and maintain it safely. Look at the following checklist. If you can tick 'Yes' for everything, you are probably using electrical equipment safely. If you are not sure about anything, you may need to ask a qualified electrician to come in to check your equipment or contact the manufacturers for advice on how to use it safely.

THE ELECTRICITY AT WORK REGULATIONS 1989

The Electricity at Work Regulations 1989 specify the ways in which electrical systems and equipment must be installed and maintained in order to prevent injury

> Did **you know...?**
>
> During 2002, faulty appliances and leads caused 6,200 fires. A further 4,800 fires were caused by misuse of equipment or appliances. Figures quoted exclude dwellings statistics.
>
> *Source: DTLR: Fire Statistics UK 2000 Report*

Checklist: Using electrical equipment safely

	Yes	Not sure	No
Do you and any staff know how to use all electrical equipment safely?			
Is all electrical equipment checked and serviced by a qualified electrician regularly (at least annually)?			
Are the service records up to date?			
Are all wires fully insulated within the plugs?			
Do you always keep water away from electrical equipment?			
Are you confident that there are no cracked plugs, frayed or bare wires, trailing wires, or loose dials or knobs on your equipment?			
Do you always check equipment on yourself before using it on a client?			

or death. Under the regulations, systems and equipment must be checked by a qualified electrician, and staff must be trained in their correct and safe use.

END POINTS

- Your salon should be equipped with the correct fire-fighting equipment.
- There are different kinds of fire extinguishers for different kinds of fire – be sure you have the correct equipment.
- Your local fire safety officer will be willing to give you advice on what equipment you need and where you should put it.
- Be sure you know what to do in case of fire – and that your staff know too.
- Under the Fire Precautions Act 1971, employers have a duty to provide a fire escape and, depending on the building, to have a fire certificate.
- If you use electrical equipment it is important to install, use, store and maintain it safely.

Topic 7 Infections and hygiene

Hygiene is a serious business for anyone working in healthcare or therapy. With any kind of personal treatment, there is always the risk of infection – to or from clients – and so it is important to be aware of infections and the way in which they are passed on.

This topic looks at the main infections to be aware of, how they are spread, and how hygiene can prevent them spreading. The next topic looks at sterilisation and waste disposal.

HOW INFECTIONS SPREAD

Infections are spread by touch, food and water, droplets in the air, and through cuts, grazes and any other incisions in the skin, such as an injection by a needle.

Although it is almost impossible to create an environment that is completely sterile, you can reduce the risk of infection by:

- avoiding treatment of people who have obvious infections

- maintaining very high standards of hygiene

- sterilising equipment

- disposing of waste safely.

What infections might spread in a treatment room or salon?

There are a number of different kinds of infection that might spread in a treatment

Type of infection	Characteristics	How it spreads	Examples
Bacterial	Caused by bacteria, single-celled micro-organisms	Bacteria reproduce at the site of infection	Skin infections like impetigo (*Staphylococcus aureus*) Throat infections (*Staphylococcus pyogens*) Food poisoning (*Salmonella*)
Viral	Caused by viruses, micro-organisms smaller than bacteria	Virus reproduces inside the human cell	Common cold Cold sore (*Herpes simplex*) Chicken pox (*Herpes zoster*) Wart (*verrucae*) Hepatitis A and B HIV
Fungal	Caused by parasitic growth; includes moulds, rusts, yeasts and mushrooms	Fungus is reproduced by spores	Ringworm (*Tinea pedis, capitis* or *corporus*) Thrush (*Candida albicans*)

room or salon. The table on the previous page summarises the main ones to be aware of, explains how they spread, and gives examples.

How can infections spread during treatment?

When an infection is spread it is called **cross-infection**. There are three main ways that infections can spread during treatment:

- via the skin through an open cut, wound or an incision, e.g. impetigo
- by breathing in droplets containing a virus, e.g. common cold
- by directly passing on a parasite or another infestation, e.g. scabies or head lice.

The first way is only likely to happen if you use a syringe, or if you or a patient has an open cut or wound. The second and third are possible whatever kind of treatment you are giving.

Blood transmitted infections

Two very serious viral infections are carried via the bloodstream and can be transmitted through cuts, wounds or incisions in the skin – **hepatitis** (**B** and **C**) and **HIV**.

Hepatitis causes inflammation of the liver and leads to jaundice, weakening the liver. It is difficult to treat and recovery can take a long time.

HIV (Human Immunodeficiency Virus) weakens the immune system and makes the person vulnerable to other infections that we can usually fight off. Someone whose immune system is badly damaged by HIV is said to have AIDS (Acquired Immune Deficiency Syndrome). Some people with HIV do not go on to develop AIDS, but those who do eventually die from infections, although with modern drug regimes, life expectancy can be greatly increased.

If your work puts you at risk of blood transmitted infections, you may want to be vaccinated against hepatitis B. There is no vaccination against hepatitis C or HIV.

HYGIENE

June is a massage therapist. She has had her own clinic for five years. Last year she was shocked to discover that she had caught ringworm. She thought it must have been from a client but couldn't remember seeing ringworm on anyone.

She decided to have a really thorough check of her hygiene procedures. She drew up a checklist and now she uses it every three months to make sure she is keeping up her own standards.

She also felt she needed to look again at the way in which she 'screened' clients to make sure they didn't have any obvious infections. Of course, she had to do this sensitively – so as well as a visual check, she decided to use a short questionnaire with each new client. She also added a short reminder to her 'welcome pack', asking clients to talk to her if they think they might have an infection.

On the opposite page is the checklist that June drew up for herself. Try using it yourself to test your own standards of hygiene. Add any other questions you can think of at the bottom.

If you answered 'Yes' to all the questions, you probably have very high standards of hygiene and you should be keeping the risk of cross-infection to the minimum. If you answered 'No' or 'Not sure' to any questions, you may need to review your hygiene procedures. You can get advice and information from the Health and

Checklist: Reducing the risk of infection

Do you always...?	Yes	Not sure	No
wash your hands before and after giving any treatment			
ask clients to wash their hands before treatments			
avoid touching any open wounds, cuts or abrasions on clients' skin – any open wounds must be covered with a plaster			
avoid breathing directly over a client			
provide a shower for clients before treatments if appropriate			
change towels and bedlinen for every client (or use disposable paper ones)			
store clean towels and bedlinen in a closed cupboard or laundry bin			
dispose of paper roll, tissues and other used material immediately in a covered container			
empty waste bins daily and disinfect them			
dispose of any glass or needles in a sharps container			
clean floors regularly – with a disinfectant if necessary			
clean toilets, washbasins and worktops regularly with disinfectant			

Checklist: Personal hygiene

Do you...?	Yes	Not sure	No
wear the correct outfit for your work and keep it clean			
shower or bath regularly			
change your underwear daily			
use antiperspirants or deodorants			
clean your teeth morning and night			
wash your hair regularly			
keep your hair tidy and away from your face or collar			
keep your fingernails short, clean and free from varnish			
never wear jewellery during treatment sessions			
wash your hands before and after treatments			

Safety Executive, whose details are included in Section 5, and also from your professional organisation.

You might also like to think about a questionnaire that you could use with new clients to help you identify any infections. Information on notifiable diseases is included in Section 2, Topic 10. Do keep a list of these handy and remind yourself of the symptoms associated with them.

Personal hygiene

Your own personal hygiene is really important, not only because it is professional and gives clients confidence, but also because it helps to ensure that you don't pass infections on. Look at the checklist at the bottom of the previous page.

Most of these things are common sense – but they can make all the difference. They are all aspects of providing a professional service to clients, and also help to protect you from disease.

END POINTS

- Infections are spread by touch, food and water, droplets in the air, and through cuts, grazes and any other incisions in the skin, such as an injection by a needle.

- You should take all possible steps to avoid the spread of infections.

- High standards of personal hygiene are essential, and are part of being professional about your work.

Topic 8 Sterilisation and waste disposal

Sterilisation methods and waste disposal are important elements of some businesses. How much you will need to think about this will depend on the kind of business you are running. For example, if you do aromatherapy or massage, sterilisation is likely to be less of an issue than if you are a beauty therapist or acupuncturist. Generally speaking, it is up to you to know what level of sterilisation you need for the different kinds of treatment or therapy you are offering.

'I'm a beauty therapist and I do electrolysis and waxing. I thought I would have to buy a lot of expensive stuff to keep my equipment sterilised. But I mainly use good quality sterilising fluids which act against viruses, fungi and bacteria, and keep them sterile in an ultraviolet cabinet which only cost around £125. It's worth every penny – you just can't risk infections.'

Meera, beauty therapist

CLEANING AND DISINFECTION

It is important to understand the differences between *cleaning*, *disinfecting* and *sterilising*, and also to know whether an item must be sterilised before use, or simply disinfected.

Disinfection is a process that reduces the number of micro-organisms to a level where infection is unlikely to occur. All equipment used for hairdressing, skin penetration, and beauty and natural therapy should be cleaned and disinfected. Items used to penetrate the skin should also be **sterilised** between clients.

Cleaning prior to disinfecting
Cleaning is vital prior to disinfecting utensils, as it prevents any build-up of organic material (hair, grease, etc.) which

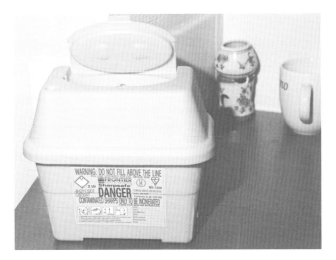

might prevent the disinfectant from working effectively.

Instruments that can be immersed in water should be cleaned in the following manner:

* washed in cold water with soap or a suitable detergent
* dried with a clean cloth
* sterilised whenever possible, or disinfected if not.

Disinfection
The procedure used for disinfecting depends on the type of disinfectant and instrument. It is therefore important to follow manufacturer's instructions, e.g. about how to dilute the disinfectant or how long to immerse objects.

Chemicals that are appropriate for disinfecting utensils include:

* alcohol, ethyl 70%
* alcohol, isopropyl 70%
* hospital-grade disinfectant
* sodium hypochlorite 1%.

Immersion containers used for disinfection should be changed daily and scrubbed out to remove any build up of organic matter that will reduce the effectiveness of the disinfectant.

Electric clippers and other metal or electrical items should not be immersed in water. Cleaning and disinfection should instead occur by wiping them with an alcohol-impregnated cotton pad to remove all 'dirt', then spraying or wiping them with an appropriate alcohol-based disinfectant.

STERILISING EQUIPMENT

Items that are required to be *sterile* are those which are used to pierce or penetrate the skin, such as tattoo needles, ear piercing studs, electrolysis needles or acupuncture needles and their associated devices.

An additional precaution is always to use sterile disposable single-use needles or penetrating items (sharps). Before sterilisation, equipment should be cleaned.

1 **Rinse** the equipment in cold water to

When cleaning items, you should wear disposable (*and durable*) gloves and protective clothing.

Needles should be visually inspected for damage before cleaning. Using a clean nylon brush or pad in the cleaning stage will help to remove material.

Sterilisation methods

There are three main methods of sterilising equipment:

- **radiation** – ultra violet (UV)
- **heat** – hot air, hot bead/glass bead, boiling, autoclave
- **chemical** – chemicals include 2% glutaraldehyde, 6% hydrogen peroxide, peracetic acid, chlorine compounds, alcohols, idophors, phenolics.

Cleaning penetration equipment prior to sterilisation

Rinse in cold water →	Wash with hot water and soap/ detergent →	Rinse in hot water →	Dry →	Sterilise and store

remove any blood or serum. (Using hot water may cause substances to coagulate and adhere to the instrument thereby preventing complete sterilisation.)

2 **Wash** the equipment using hot water and soap or detergent.

3 **Rinse** the equipment thoroughly in hot water (greater than 70°C) and allow to **dry**.

4 **Sterilise** the equipment using an approved steriliser (see below).

5 **Store** under cover in a clean, dry and dust-free environment.

Look at the different sterilisation options in the chart on the opposite page. While you are reading through the chart, think about whether you will need to use any methods of sterilisation in your business and if so, which ones.

Ultraviolet cabinets should not be relied upon to disinfect or sterilise items, as the radiation does not penetrate to all surfaces of the articles exposed. They should mainly be used for storage of clean and disinfected items.

Method	What it can be used for	Advantages	Disadvantages
UV cabinet – UV rays are emitted from a special bulb in a cabinet	Storing already clean objects after they have been sterilised in an autoclave or chemical solution, e.g. tweezers, manicure items.	Stores instruments in a clean environment	UV rays only travel in straight lines. Instruments must be turned so all surfaces are cleansed. Any debris, oil or dust on the object prevents the UV from working
Hot air oven	Penetrates water-soluble materials (e.g. grease and oil) and can be used for glassware, instruments or containers.	Less corrosive to metals and sharp instruments than steam	Loading and packing must be done very carefully Takes 2–4 hours
Hot bead/glass bead cabinet – objects are placed in a container of small glass beads which are heated to high temperatures	Small metal objects that cannot be damaged by heat, e.g. forceps, tweezers, etc.	Safe, and reasonably fast	Only suitable for small items. May cause metal instruments to discolour and distort
Boiling – for five minutes after boiling point reached	Most useful for laundry and other cloth items, such as towels and headbands.	Fast Most forms of bacteria are destroyed after five minutes of boiling	Some spores and viruses may not be destroyed by boiling
Autoclave (steam cabinet) – produces steam under pressure in enclosed cabinet	'High risk' metal instruments: tweezers, etc. Decontamination of reusable supplies and infectious waste.	Can destroy all micro-organisms and spores. Most dependable form of sterilisation. Fast	Loading and packing is critical Damages heat-sensitive items Maintenance and quality control are essential More expensive
Chemical sterilisation – (min 70% alcohol) wash and then soak instruments in solution. Dry and store in clean environment.	Most objects, including those that are intolerant to heat, including tweezers, forceps, pedicure equipment, scissors.	Easy to obtain Inexpensive	Risk of spillage Cheaper solutions (including bleach) may cause items to discolour or corrode Must change fluid regularly

Sterilising your equipment

Now make a list of the type or types of sterilisation that you will need for your business. Remember to choose the methods that do what you want most effectively and economically. There is no need to 'over-sterilise' – you just need to reach the right level of cleanliness for each object.

You must have all your sterilisation equipment and procedures in place before you start running your business, as you will need them from day one.

WASTE DISPOSAL

It goes almost without saying that bins should have closed lids. Bags should be emptied and bins disinfected daily.

The other important aspect of keeping infections to a minimum is disposing of waste safely. Local councils have regulations covering disposal of waste. Glass and sharp items need special handling. As this may vary from authority to authority, you should find out what is appropriate in your area.

Needles

If you work with needles – or 'sharps' as they are also known – the most important hazard is the transmission of blood-borne infections such as hepatitis or HIV (see Section 3, Topic 7). For disposing of needles you will need a 'sharps container'. It must:

- be durable

- be leak resistant

- be puncture resistant

- have a lockable lid.

Sharps boxes must be removed and replaced before they are full. They should

never be emptied as there is a significant risk to individuals from hepatitis. As these items are cheap to replace, it is appropriate to replace the box and contact a disposal expert to collect the old one.

Be very careful when disposing of needles. Keep the sharps container in a safe place where it can't be reached by clients or children. Anyone who works with you will need to know what it is and how to use it.

'I never empty my sharps containers. I just take the full box with all used needles to the local hospital for disposal.'

Maria, acupuncturist

If you need or want to know more about sterilisation, some suggestions of books and articles are included in the Resources section at the end of this book. Make sure you are familiar with the terms relating to hygiene and sterilisation, which you should have learned during your training.

END POINTS

- You need to know the differences between cleaning, disinfecting and sterilising, and whether an item must be sterilised before use or simply disinfected.

- Cleaning is vital prior to disinfecting utensils.

- Disinfection is a process that reduces the number of micro-organisms to a level where infection is unlikely to occur.

- Items used to penetrate the skin should be sterilised between clients.

- Choose the methods of cleaning, disinfection and sterilisation suitable for your business.

- You must follow the local council regulations on waste disposal.

- Special care must be taken in the safe disposal of 'sharps'.

Topic 9 Security

Anyone running a business needs to be aware of security. If you are running a salon or clinic you will need to think about the security of:

- clients
- staff
- equipment
- stock
- cash
- records
- the building
- yourself.

'I learnt my lesson early on. I had just opened the clinic and had spent the previous month decorating it and making it look good. We had been open for about two weeks when we were burgled on the Sunday evening. Apart from taking the computer and some other equipment, they completely trashed the place, pouring oils everywhere, smearing creams on the mirrors and walls. It was awful. After that I had closed-circuit cameras and a burglar alarm installed. It was expensive but worth it. We haven't had any trouble since.'

Neil, sports therapist

DOING A SECURITY ASSESSMENT

It's worth starting by doing a thorough check of how secure your business is. Try to do this at least once a year to make sure you are not at any new security risk and that all the measures you have taken are still effective. Work through the checklist on the following page to determine how safe and secure the place where you work is.

This is a long list and may seem overwhelming at first, but try to work through it steadily. Any time or money you spend now will almost certainly save

you time and money in the long run. If you answered 'No' or 'Not sure' to any questions, you may need to invest in some additional security measures. Contact your local community safety officer for information and practical advice.

Read through the case study that follows to see what security issues Karen, a beauty therapist just starting up in business, will have to deal with.

Karen opened a small beauty salon six months ago. She runs it on her own with one part-time assistant, Carmen, who works every afternoon.

The salon is located in the centre of a suburban town, down a poorly lit side alley. It has one treatment room, a toilet, and a small storeroom. The toilet can be locked but the storeroom can't. There is a glazed front door with an ordinary lock, a back door with a lock and two bolts, and three windows without window locks.

Karen has lots of equipment in the salon including:

- *a computer for appointments and record keeping*
- *a microcurrent face- and body-lifting machine*

Checklist: Security assessment

	Yes	Not sure	No
Are staff and clients safe in your salon (Section 3, Topic 1)?			
Are staff aware of security issues and procedures?			
Do you have secure locks on all doors and windows?			
Do you have any other necessary security equipment, such as a burglar alarm, security lights, closed-circuit cameras?			
Are doorways well lit day and night?			
Do you limit the amount of cash or jewellery that you and other staff bring to work?			
Is there somewhere secure to put cash or jewellery, e.g. lockers or a locked room with limited access to the key?			
Are expensive products and equipment kept under lock and key, with limited access to the key?			
Do you store parts of equipment, e.g. leads and attachments separately?			
Do you security mark and number all equipment and check it regularly?			
Is the till or cash box kept locked and away from the door, and emptied overnight?			
Do you have a notice on the front door or window to say that no cash is left overnight in the building?			
Do you plan staff rotas and appointments so that female staff are not working alone in the salon?			
If you have products on display, do you use dummies not the real thing?			
Do you store confidential records in a locked filing cabinet, with limited access to the key?			
Do you use a password on your computer to restrict access to confidential data?			
If you have to go to the bank with money, do you vary the time and route?			
If you bank a lot of money, do you use a security firm?			
Does your insurance cover cash?			
Do you avoid booking appointments when you are alone in the house, clinic or salon?			
Do you leave a record of home visits with someone else?			

• laser hair removal equipment

• depilation equipment.

She keeps products for treatments in the storeroom. Products for sale to clients are kept on a shelf at the back of the salon.

Karen banks her takings just before she shuts the salon while Carmen is still working. The bank is a two-minute walk away in the High Street.

Her main deliveries of stock arrive on Thursday mornings. Because Karen is on her own in the salon, she leaves the back door unlocked that morning and the delivery person leaves the boxes just inside the back door.

The business is going well and Karen has started opening until 9pm on Tuesdays to fit in clients who work during the day. Carmen doesn't work in the evenings.

Security advice

Think about Karen's salon from a security point of view. What do you think she could do to make her salon (and herself) as secure as possible?

There are a few fairly easy things Karen could do to make her salon more secure.

- Add lighting to the entrance to the salon.

- Put a security light at the front and back of the building.

- Install a device that rings or buzzes every time the front door opens – so that she knows someone has come in when she is not in the front of the building.

- Put an additional lock on the front door and change the glass to security glazing.

- Use a five-lever mortice lock (many insurance companies insist on this).

- Put window locks on all the windows.

- Put a lock on the storeroom so that she

can keep valuables, treatment products, expensive equipment and confidential records there. Keep products for sale to clients there too, and put dummies on the shelf at the back of the salon. Get a spare key to keep at home in case she loses the main key for the storeroom.

- Ask Carmen to come in too on Tuesday evenings so that she isn't working alone. If Carmen can't work, recruit someone else to be there.

- Be cautious about booking appointments for when she is alone in the salon – ensure they are clients she knows.

- Security mark all expensive equipment – she could use a special marker pen or electronic tagging.

- Store equipment in the storeroom but keep leads and attachments somewhere else.

- Vary the time when she banks the money, and use a different route sometimes if possible.

- Change the stock delivery time to an afternoon when Carmen is there. Check that all boxes contain the correct stock before the delivery person leaves.

As her business expands, she might want to consider:

- installing a burglar alarm
- installing closed-circuit cameras
- employing another part-time assistant in the mornings to ensure that there are always at least two members of staff working at any time
- using a security firm to take the money to the bank
- introducing more complex stock control procedures to ensure that stock cannot be stolen by staff or clients.

END POINTS

- You should carry out regular security assessments to check that the place where you work is a safe and secure environment.
- There are security implications relating to all the following: people (you, staff and clients), the building, equipment, stock, cash, confidential client records.

Topic 10 Stock control

If you are running any business that carries stock, you need to know about stock control: knowing what you've got in stock and when to order fresh supplies. Good stock control means never running out of anything, but also not having lots of unused supplies sitting on shelves. Your stock might be both professional products for your salon, and retail products for customers.

KNOWING HOW MUCH STOCK YOU'VE GOT

'It took me a long time to get it right with the stock control. I was so worried that I would run out of the tints I use on my clients that I kept ordering too much. Then I sat down and thought about it. The supplier often delivered on the day I ordered and the most I ever have to wait is one day.

So I started doing a quick check of stock each Thursday, looking ahead to the next week and making any orders on the Friday morning before my first appointment. That way I have everything I need by the Monday morning. I also negotiated with the supplier to pay on a monthly account, so I'm not spending money before it comes in.'

Valerie, hairdresser

There are several ways of knowing how much stock you've got. What you do will depend on the nature of your work and the kind of supplies you use.

If you don't use many different kinds of supplies, you might be able simply to keep an eye on what you've got left – daily, weekly or monthly, depending on how quickly you use the supplies. For example, if you use bottles of aromatherapy oils, you could keep them in rows, five or six bottles deep. You will know you are running out of any bottles by looking to see which rows

are nearly at the back of the shelf.

For other kinds of supplies you may need to keep records, either manually or on a computer.

Manual stock control

The simplest form of manual stock control involves keeping a record card for each item.

Lorraine is an aromatherapist and she keeps a manual stock control system for the essential oils she uses in her business. She keeps one card for each oil, putting them in a rotary card index. The record card shows:

- *what the item is*
- *how much she has in stock on what date*
- *when her last order was*
- *when she needs to order more.*

On the last weekend of every month she goes through the card index and lists all the oils she needs to order for the next month.

Another simple way of keeping track of stock is to head up a piece of paper with the name and contact details of each company that supplies products you stock (e.g. Clarins, Decleor, etc.). Then, each month (or however often you take stock) write down the item(s), how many you have in stock and how many you need to order. An example is shown on the next page.

Product	April 6		May 4		June 4	
	How many in stock	How many to order	How many in stock	How many to order	How many in stock	How many to order
Cleanser – dry	0	2	1	1	0	3
Toner – dry	3	1	3	0	1	2
Day cream	1	1	0	2	0	3
Night cream	2	0	0	2	1	2

Make sure to include a note of the date you take stock and order new items. This will help you to see whether you are ordering too often or not often enough.

Most salons and clinics need to place an order every 4–6 weeks, depending on the size of the salon of course. Large companies such as Decleor and Clarins are likely to visit the salon on a monthly basis, but smaller companies will leave it to the salon to order stocks when necessary.

Computerised stock control

The method outlined above could easily be implemented on a computer, either as an Excel spreadsheet or as a simple Word document. If your stock control is more complex than this, or you prefer to work on a computer, you may want to invest in a computer software package with stock control features, e.g. Sage or Quickbooks. It's a good idea to get some demonstration software first to try out the packages and decide which is right for you.

Think about how complex your stock control will be and try to make a judgement now about what kind of system you might need to use:

• regular visual checks

• manual record system

• computerised record system.

The best stock control system is the simplest one that works for you.

WHEN TO ORDER FRESH SUPPLIES

An effective stock control system has to be based on knowing how quickly you are likely to run out of stock. Of course, when you first set up your business you won't have this information – you will have to monitor how you use supplies to find this out. Keeping a record as explained above will give you this information.

Ryan is a sports therapist at a local gym. For his work he uses ultrasound. For his stock control he uses a computer software package. When he bought the software he worked out his rate of usage for gels and oil so that the software could automatically flag up anything that was going into short supply. Every two days he runs the program to check on his stock. The computer printout tells him what he needs to order, initially within two days and also over the next week or so.

Try to keep a record for a month or two and then analyse your average usage –

daily, weekly or monthly depending on how fast you are getting through supplies. Bear in mind the time taken for delivery – you can probably adjust your system so that you order stock when you have one week's supply left.

Keep your staff involved in controlling stock levels as they have a good idea of how quickly things sell and, if they are on a commission scheme, an interest in ensuring that there is always a product to sell.

Your consumption of supplies will depend on the nature of your work and how many clients you have, but you should be able to work out when you need to order fresh supplies by following these basic principles.

ROTATING STOCK

If you go into any supermarket, you can see how they keep their stock moving by putting new items at the back of the shelf and bringing the older products forward. That way they can make sure products do not go past their 'best before' date. It's important for you to keep your stock moving like this too.

If you find that slow-moving products are going past their 'best before' date, then you should consider reducing stock levels, or possibly telling clients that you will order specially for them.

If you sell products to clients, keep an eye on which products sell quickly, and make sure you don't run out of them or you will lose a potential sale. What sells quickly may vary, perhaps with the seasons, so you may need to be flexible enough in your ordering systems to reflect this.

END POINTS

- If your business carries stock, you need to know about stock control – making sure you know what you've got in stock and when to order fresh supplies.

- The simplest form of manual stock control, suitable if you stock very few items, involves keeping a record card for each item or company.

- Computerised stock control systems are also available.

- Stock rotation ensures that older stock is used before newer stock.

- Include staff in stock control, especially to ensure that items are logged as sold. Commission on sales encourages staff to keep more careful track of stock!

This topic looks at managing reception and making appointments for clients. First impressions really count, so giving clients a good reception is vital. Managing appointments efficiently is also essential – you can lose a lot of time and goodwill if your appointment system doesn't run smoothly.

'I really enjoy greeting clients and having a little chat with them. When I started to expand my hair dressing business I found it hard to find staff who took the same approach. I suppose it wasn't their business so they didn't have the same interest. However, I eventually found a wonderful person, Sally, who now manages the whole reception and appointments area beautifully. She had worked in a busy GP practice before, so it is impossible to fluster her. The clients really like her and the whole atmosphere is really welcoming.'

Lorraine, owner of a hairdressing salon

FIRST IMPRESSIONS

Look at this picture of a reception area in a physiotherapy centre. Find all the things that are wrong with it.

This is just about as bad as it gets! Hopefully, your own reception area is nothing like this.

Have a quick check now of how efficient and welcoming your reception is by working through the checklist on the next page.

Checklist: How good is your reception?

	Yes	Not sure	No
Is your reception area clean, attractive and welcoming?			
Do you always give clients a friendly welcome when they come in? Do you use their names and put them at their ease?			
Do you and your staff always look clean, tidy and professional?			
When you and your staff answer the telephone, do you always sound friendly and interested?			
Are all client records kept confidential in the reception area?			
Do staff on reception know enough about treatments and/or products to give clients some basic advice when they first come in?			
Do you make sure that no one gossips in the reception area?			
Are information sheets available?			
Do all staff attend updating sessions on products and treatments?			
Have reception staff had training in 'professionalism', e.g. confidentiality, not answering or asking personal questions, etc?			

You should be able to answer 'Yes' to all these questions. These things are just as important whether you cover reception yourself or employ other people to do this for you. A good reception for clients can make the difference between a thriving business and a failing business.

If you employ staff to deal with reception and appointments, it is important to give them a solid grounding in the nature of the treatments and products you offer. You can find out more about training courses from local further or higher education institutions or private colleges. Some larger companies offer training in product knowledge, which can be extremely helpful.

Knowing who your next client is, when they are due to arrive, and what treatment they are booked in for will help you to prepare for them and greet them appropriately.

Taking payments

In some clinics and centres, clients pay for their treatment or therapy at reception. If this is the case, you or other staff will need to know how to use a till or how to log payments manually. You will need a record of all payments received so that you can balance your books.

'At first I took payments from clients in the treatment room as soon as their sessions finished. That was fine when I only had a few clients, but as I got more, I found it too difficult to keep track of the money that was coming in. You need to keep things in order for your accounts. So I started to do the money things separately downstairs so that I could write everything in a proper cash book.'

Dorothy, manager of natural health clinic

MAKING APPOINTMENTS

A good appointment system is essential for the smooth running of a centre or clinic. You can keep track of appointments manually, with an appointment book, or on a computer, using a software program.

Manual appointment systems

Manual appointment systems usually revolve around an appointments book. If you work on your own, this will be relatively easy to keep because you will be the only person using it. If you work with others, you will all have to use it in the same way so that confusion doesn't arise. It's best to write appointments in pencil, so that cancelled appointments can be rubbed out and new appointments can be clearly written in.

Computer appointment systems

Computer appointment systems are becoming increasingly popular. There are a number of different software programs to choose from – your professional organisation may be able to point you in the right direction. If you work on your own, you can also use the computer system to add notes about clients, e.g. 'Seemed a bit anxious last time'. However, if you are keeping computerised records about clients, you will need to be aware of confidentiality issues, and you may need to register with the Data Protection Registrar (see Topic 3 in this section).

Taking telephone appointments

Although some clients will make their next appointment at the end of their session, many will want to phone for an appointment. When taking telephone appointments, be welcoming and helpful, and having agreed on the time and day of the appointment, read it back to the client to double check that neither of you has made a mistake. Make sure you add it to the appointments book or computer system while you are talking to the client – it's easy to forget afterwards!

END POINTS

- First impressions really count, so it is vital to give clients a good reception when they come to you.

- The reception area should be attractive, while reception staff should be professional, well-presented and attentive to clients' needs.

- A good appointment system is essential for the smooth running of a centre or clinic.

Topic 12 Dealing with difficulties

This topic looks at some of the difficulties you might face once your business is up and running, and how to avoid them, focusing on:

- problems with payment from clients
- missed appointments
- orders that don't arrive.

These are three of the most common difficulties a small business can face, and we will look at ways of dealing with them. The skills that you need to deal with these difficulties may well be transferable to other issues that you face in your business, but some problems will always require specialist help. If in doubt, try contacting your professional association for guidance.

PROBLEMS WITH PAYMENT

If your clients always pay by cash, you shouldn't have any problems with this aspect of your business. At the very outset, tell clients your fee and outline the cost of any products or prescriptions, and make it clear that you expect to be paid at the end of each session. You can either do this over the phone, tactfully, or send out a written information sheet (including directions) before the first appointment.

'I avoided offering a credit card facility at first because I knew you had to pay the credit card company each time you used it. But for big amounts, I think it is worth

paying for the peace of mind. I don't take credit card payments for less than £15.'

Lorena, complementary therapist

If clients pay by credit card, the credit company guarantees payment to you, although you do have to pay a fee for each transaction to cover this. You don't have to offer clients this facility if the size of your business doesn't really warrant it.

'I was shocked to find that a client I had been seeing for three years, who seemed totally trustworthy, had written me a cheque that later bounced. She didn't come to the centre again – she must have known what she was doing. Now I always insist on a cheque card, however well I know – or think I know – the client.'

Stewart, physiotherapist

Checklist: Payments by cheque

When you receive a cheque, do you always check that:	Yes	Not sure	No
the cheque has been made out correctly and signed			
there is an accompanying cheque card			
the cheque card is still valid			
the cheque card guarantees the amount on the cheque			
you (not the client) write the cheque card number on the back of the cheque?			

You should have answered 'Yes' to all these questions. If you make these simple checks every time you are given a cheque, you shouldn't have any problem with bouncing cheques.

If clients pay by cheque or credit card, you will have to be more careful and make sure that you have systems to avoid cheques 'bouncing'. It is quite possible for a client to write a cheque for their treatment when they know they don't have enough in their bank account. If they don't have an overdraft facility at the bank, the bank will 'bounce' the cheque, i.e. send it back to them without transferring the money to you.

MISSED APPOINTMENTS

If clients don't turn up for their appointments, you can really lose out financially. When an appointment is made, you set aside time for that particular client, and you can't see another client during that time. If the client fails to turn up, you lose that income. A small business simply cannot afford to have time when there is no income.

To avoid the difficulty of missed appointments, decide what your arrangements are for cancellations. For example, you might decide that clients can cancel within 24 hours of an appointment (you might have time to re-fill the slot) but after that you will charge the whole fee. Whatever you decide, let all clients know what the arrangements are and keep to them, however genuine a client's difficulty might be.

Most clinics or salons maintain a 'client cancellation list' of clients who can be contacted to offer them a cancelled appointment, sometimes at a discount.

'People come up with such sob stories. I used to just say "Don't worry." But I found with all the missed appointments I was losing so much money. You have to be business-like – make it clear to clients what your rules on missed appointments are and stick to them. Most clients are happy to go along with you if you explain the reasons.'

Moira, owner of a beauty salon

ORDERS THAT DON'T ARRIVE

Michelle runs a home hairdressing service. She gets through a lot of towels each week and uses a local laundry to wash them – with three small children, she doesn't have time to deal with the laundry herself. She pays the laundry on a monthly account. The laundry has always been totally reliable, but one Monday, after a change of manager, her delivery of towels fails to arrive. She can't work without the towels. What should she do?

Michelle can't afford to lose any of her clients so she must act quickly to get the clean towels from the laundry. She should start by telephoning the manager to find out what has happened and when the towels are likely to be delivered. If she doesn't get a satisfactory answer, she should contact the owner of the business to report the problem. She should make it clear to the owner that she will be buying new towels and will be charging the laundry for the cost unless her own towels are delivered within four hours (a reasonable time to wash, dry and deliver towels).

If an order fails to arrive, you may not be able to work. To avoid this happening, it's worth setting up an ordering procedure so that you have a record of:

• what you ordered

• when you ordered it

• who your contact at the company is.

If you have a record of what you ordered and when, you have something to refer to if a delivery fails to turn up. If you have a contact name you know who to get in touch with as soon as there is a problem.

Make sure you check incoming orders immediately. Some companies will only accept responsibility for missing items for 24 hours after delivery.

You might want to devise an order form that you can send out with every order confirming price and quantity.

Only use reputable suppliers and try to establish a good business relationship with them so that they are less likely to let you down. Don't pay upfront if you can help it – ask for an invoice with your order.

It is a good idea to ask for samples of new products to test before you purchase anything. Also, get to know the local rep – if you need supplies urgently, the local rep can usually help.

DEALING WITH COMPLAINTS

You need to be aware of your professional body's complaints procedure (we have looked at this in Section 2) and be prepared to initiate the process if you receive a complaint. This is one very good reason for belonging to a professional body that has a complaints procedure!

If you work in a multi-disciplinary clinic, make sure there is a generic complaints procedure clearly displayed. This should ensure that all therapists agree to work to a common ethical standard, and if the clinic receives a complaint, there is a procedure to deal with this.

END POINTS

- Decide what methods of payment you will accept and let clients know this at the start.

- Only accept cheques when guaranteed by a cheque card.

- To avoid the difficulty of clients missing or cancelling appointments, decide what your arrangements are for cancellations and make sure that clients know what they are.

- To avoid the problem of orders not being met, only use reputable suppliers and try to establish a good business relationship with them.

Section 4

Business development and marketing

Topic 1 Marketing

Marketing is critical to the success of any business – whether it's a one-person operation, medium-sized company or a multinational corporation. For small businesses, it's even more important to get the marketing right as they cannot afford to get it wrong. Remember that everything you do, and the way you do it, is all marketing – doing something well is usually just as easy as doing it badly, but wins you a good reputation.

WHAT IS MARKETING?

The Chartered Institute of Marketing defines marketing as: *'The management process which identifies, anticipates and supplies customer requirements efficiently and profitably.'*

So marketing is not just about advertising and selling products or services, but about:

* finding out what potential customers want

* creating products and services that satisfy those needs
* selling those products and services at the right price
* making those products and services available in the right place.

Are you doing all of these?

Checklist: Getting the product right

Does your product meet your customers' needs?	☐ It is perfectly suited to customers and no changes are needed
	☐ Some changes may be needed
	☐ Not sure – I'd have to find out
How do your products compare with your competitors'?	☐ Ours are better
	☐ Reasonably well
	☐ Not very well
	☐ Don't know
Every product or service can be said to have a four-stage life cycle. Where are your products or services in the life cycle?	☐ Birth – a new product is launched and introduced to prospective customers
	☐ Growth – the product becomes popular and starts to sell well
	☐ Maturity – the product is selling so well we can't keep up
	☐ Decline – demand and sales fall. Customers turn their attention elsewhere

HOW YOU ARE DOING?

The four elements of marketing are known as the **four Ps** – Product, Price, Promotion and Place. Use the checklists to see how well you are doing on each of the four Ps.

The product

The product can be:

- tangible goods, e.g. a bottle of aromatherapy oil, or a support bandage

- a service, e.g. a massage, manicure, or therapy session.

The price

The price should be:

- thought to be fair by the customer – not necessarily the cheapest, but value for money

- competitive – so that when customers compare your prices to your competitors', they think yours are within the price range they would expect to pay

- profitable – unless you are trading at a profit, you won't last any longer than your overdraft facility. The price for each hour of treatment must cover rent, rates, light, heating, wages, telephones, consumables, leased equipment, repairs, maintenance, advertising, promotions, accountant's fees, insurance, travel and your time – and still provide a profit. Refer to your professional organisation for guidelines on costing treatments.

Checklist: Getting the price right

Have you worked out the right price for your product?	☐ I've included all costs and come up with an appropriate price
	☐ Hmm – I'm still working on this
	☐ I'm not sure – I've never really gone into it
How do your prices compare with your competitors'?	☐ Competitive
	☐ Much cheaper
	☐ Much more expensive
	☐ Don't know
Does the price you charge represent value for money?	☐ Yes
	☐ Not really, but we can't afford to charge less

'When I started up by myself, I was a bit nervous about how much I could charge – so I charged about 25% less than the local salon. After about a year, when things had properly got going, I was always having to turn people away. So I raised my prices! I was worried, but my books are still full, and I'm making more money for the same amount of work.'

Jacinta, travelling nail technician

'It didn't take me long to realise that I would have to be very disciplined about keeping to time for each appointment. If you overrun, not only do you earn less, but you run the risk of annoying clients who have to wait – and they may decide to go somewhere else!'

Andi, beauty therapist

Checklist: Getting the promotion right

Have you got a promotion strategy for your products and services?

- ☐ I'm fairly confident that our promotion will give the results we want
- ☐ I'm working on it
- ☐ I need to look at how other people do it

Promotion

Promotion is how a product or service is brought to the attention of potential customers, such as:

- advertising – newspaper, journal, magazine, radio, television, billboards
- competitions – e.g. create a winning slogan and win a holiday for two
- special offers – e.g. buy one get one free; buy now pay next year; 0% interest; money-off tokens.

Checklist: Getting the place right

Where do you offer your product or services?

- ☐ Local newspapers
- ☐ Local radio
- ☐ Posters
- ☐ Talks and demonstrations
- ☐ Leaflets
- ☐ Yellow Pages and Thomson's Directory
- ☐ On our website
- ☐ Other means

The place

The place is:

- where the goods or services are offered for sale – shops, supermarkets, mail order catalogues, the Internet

- the way the goods or services are distributed and delivered to the customer.

'I got no response at all to an advert in the local newspaper, but I put an ad in the parish magazine, which was really cheap, and I've had loads of contacts asking for daytime consultations in their homes, while the kids are at school.'

Suzette, reflexologist

IMPROVING YOUR MARKETING

If your answers to the questions above indicate that you need to do better, then you need to ask yourself more questions. For example:

- if you believe your products do not compare well with your competitors, what improvements do you need to make

- are there any pricing changes you need to make

- where can you market your goods and services?

If you do not know how your products compare to your competitors', how can you find out what customers think? To find out what customers want, most companies carry out **market research**.

Primary research is the gathering of new information from existing customers and potential customers, and can be done by:

- talking to customers – face-to-face, on the phone, or by written questionnaires

- organising focus groups – getting customers together to talk about your products.

Secondary research involves looking at information already available, e.g. government statistics, published reports, etc.

Primary research is usually more expensive but is more accurate than secondary research because you can talk direct to your own customer base.

Don't just put the results of your research on a shelf. Look at what people say, and try to think of ways of addressing their concerns. You may need to change certain practices, target your marketing at a different group, or adjust the prices of your treatments.

'For a couple of weeks last year, I gave each customer a little feedback form to fill in – they could get £2 off their next treatment if they returned a completed form. Eight out of the thirteen people who returned forms said that they didn't like the way the reception desk was tucked away to the right of the main door when they came in, and that the rubbish bin outside the door was often overflowing and smelly. I hadn't noticed, but now we check the bin twice a day, and have moved the reception desk so that the receptionist is facing customers as they walk in – and it looks so much more professional.'

Dinan, sports therapist

END POINTS

- To market your product well, you must get the four Ps right – Product, Price, Promotion and Place.

- Monitor results and be prepared to change your marketing strategy, promotions or products if: products age or go out of fashion; competitors appear in your area; customers' needs change.

- Be willing to ask your customers or clients what they think, and prepared to act on the results.

Topic 2 Promotion

Most people think of promotion as advertising. Promotion is much more than this – it is about running all aspects of your business in a way that promotes your products and services. This includes your business cards, customer receipts, advertising, teeshirts, special offers, competitions and even your car.

Promotion can raise the profile of your business, and increase public awareness and knowledge of the treatments that you offer, and their benefits.

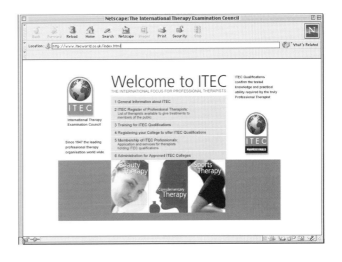

Checklist: Advertising

Do you:

- ☐ advertise in newspapers
- ☐ advertise in the parish magazine
- ☐ appear in the Yellow Pages or Thomsons directory
- ☐ run adverts on local radio
- ☐ put up posters
- ☐ understand the implications of the relevant legislation
- ☐ run workshops?

ADVERTISING

Even if you haven't thought much about promotion, you have probably thought about – even done – some advertising.

All of these can promote your business, but they need to be used appropriately. Your promotion efforts must repay you or there's no point in doing them. So, they must be *targeted* at people who either are, or may be, interested in your product. A sports therapist is more likely to get a good response to adverts in the local sports centre than the parish magazine. A nail technician might find the reverse to be true.

Whatever media you choose to use, you have to be sure that the readers or listeners will want your product, can afford your product, and can get to you to buy your product. Don't advertise your hairdressing

salon in *The Times* – it won't be cost-effective. Posters are good at attracting trade to a local business, but must be placed where your potential customers pass by.

Advertisements should always look professional, particularly when they will be compared with your competitors' adverts. They should always have your business name, contact details, and what you do. Typefaces and logos should be consistent with those on your headed paper, business cards, product or treatment leaflets, and bills and receipts.

Your professional organisation may give guidance on how to advertise your services.

'Every piece of paper now has our name, our phone number and a brief list of the treatments we offer on it. Lots of new customers call because they get our number from receipts, cards or leaflets that they've been given by existing customers.'

Michael, director of therapy centre

Legal implications

It's important to be aware of the implications of the legislation governing advertising and selling.

The Trades Descriptions Act governs any advertising you do. The Advertising Standards Authority (www.asa.org.uk) can provide information about any restrictions that may apply to you but, basically, you must accurately describe the products and services you are selling. You also need to be aware of:

The Supply of Goods and Services Act

Any goods (such as beauty products or natural remedies) must be 'of suitable quality' and be 'fit for the purpose for which they are sold'. In addition, if there are safety standards for the goods, you could be liable to criminal prosecution if you are in breach of this Act.

Consumer Protection Act

This Act covers both goods and services; there may be particular restrictions on some services and you should refer to any code of conduct for your particular profession.

Checklist: Promotion

Do you:

- [ ] print your phone number and a slogan on your receipts
- [ ] encourage word-of-mouth referrals
- [ ] send press releases to the local press
- [ ] give talks and demonstrations about your treatments or services
- [ ] have a sign on your car
- [ ] have polo shirts with the company name and logo
- [ ] always carry business cards with you, even to social functions
- [ ] do mail shots
- [ ] have a website
- [ ] run promotions, e.g. 'Bring a friend and have a half-price treatment'
- [ ] run competitions in the local press
- [ ] arrange events to promote a product or treatment, or to introduce a new therapist?

IMPROVING YOUR PROMOTION

Promotion is more than just advertising.

Your own stationery

Printing a phone number for appointments on your receipts means that there is another piece of paper with your number on it in a customer's house.

Hopefully, next time they want a massage, they will pick it up and phone you, not a competitor.

A promotional offer on your bill – e.g. 5% off the next treatment or a choice of oils – can be another incentive for them to return, or to recommend you to a friend.

The press

Sending press releases to the local newspaper when you open a new salon; qualify to give a new treatment; or do anything newsworthy can be a route to free, locally targeted publicity for your business.

You can often combine press releases about new treatments with announcements of talks or demonstrations of the new therapy. These can be effective ways of spreading the word to potential customers, either directly or by word of mouth.

You

As you travel in your car, either on business or socially, you are driving free advertising space around the area where your customers live. Use it.

Clothing can promote your business. For a sports therapist, for example, polo shirts printed with the business logo and phone number provide promotion and improve your professional presentation.

When you socialise, always carry some business cards with you as you may meet potential customers.

Mailings

Mailshots require careful consideration. The database of customers that you mail must contain a high percentage of possible customers, in the right age group, locality, income range, profession, etc.

The best way to build up a database targeted to your customers is to do it from your existing and past clients, and to mailshot them to encourage repeat or returning business, possibly combined with an incentive.

'I bought a database of names to use for a mailshot from the computer, and did a trial mailing, which cost a lot, what with post and paper and stuff. Lucky I did,

because I got no replies from two hundred letters. Then I went home one day, and picked up the post from the doormat. The first thing I always do is to bin the junk mail. That was when I realised that my mailshot needed to have been carefully targeted to people who might be interested, not just people in the area.'

Michael, director of holistic therapy centre

The web

Websites are very trendy but, like posters on a wall, are only seen by people who actually go to them. You may choose to use a website to provide contact details, directions and maps, lists of treatments, prices, etc., in such a way that customers can download them easily. However, the information on a website must be maintained and kept up to date, and you should be certain that the effort is worth the return.

'We've got a little website, but we've kept it deliberately simple so it's easy to navigate and quick to load. It provides information on what we offer, how much we charge, and how to find and contact us.'

Sian, complementary therapy practice manager

IS IT WORTH IT?

Always measure the effectiveness of promotions, so that you know whether or not they are worth doing. To do this, put a reference code on the leaflet, advert or poster for the customer to quote, then you use it to track which promotions perform best.

END POINTS

- Focus on low-cost or free promotional opportunities, including:
  - presenting yourself well
  - talks to local groups of all kinds, and people of all ages
  - short introductory courses on your particular area or as part of a team introducing complementary therapies
  - open days at your clinic or salon (try to get local press coverage), including light refreshments, demonstrations, etc.
  - taking part in local events, e.g. village fêtes, green fairs, local business networks, etc.
  - establishing positive relationships with local retail outlets connected to your therapy, e.g. local health food shop
  - networking with other health professionals.
- Your promotional activity, whether advertising, teeshirts, or special offers, must offer a product:
  - the customer is interested in buying
  - to the customer who may buy it
  - in a place where they will see it.
- All promotional activities should be cost-effective, and should be tracked so that you can tell which provides the best results.

Marketing skills help you to decide what your product should be and what you can charge. Promotion makes your customers aware of your product or service. Selling skills clinch the sale, or sell additional products.

HOW DO SELLING SKILLS HELP MY BUSINESS?

Selling skills will help you to sell retail products on the back of a service, or continuing courses of a therapy, to ensure future income. A customer who has just paid for a treatment should be a happy one, and is therefore likely to be amenable to booking their next appointment, or purchasing retail products (oils, beauty products, etc.).

Selling a course of treatment to a customer, even with a discount to encourage them, means that the client returns to your clinic – not someone else's – and pays for treatment in advance, hence improving your cash flow.

I'M A THERAPIST – WHY DO I WANT TO SELL RETAIL PRODUCTS?

Selling products to the customer links the treatment to the products. It allows and encourages customers to continue treating themselves at home between consultations. This helps maintain their interest in the treatment and makes repeat consultations more likely.

By selling retail products in the salon or centre, you can generate extra revenue for the business without taking up valuable consultation time and treatment rooms. The sale can often take place when the customer is paying for a treatment, and is a useful bridge to the subject of booking a repeat appointment.

'I always recommend a small bottle of the oils I have used to my customers at the end of a consultation. I suggest that they can continue the benefits of the treatment by using the oil at home until their next appointment. This allows me to bring up the subject of their next booking easily and without pressure.'

Shane, aromatherapist

Good displays of attractively packaged retail products can also improve the presentation and appearance of a salon or centre. As well as providing easy extra revenue at an excellent profit margin, retail sales offer an excellent opportunity to create sales incentives for staff. You could set up a 'performance-related' element to pay, by adopting a simple commission scheme so that staff earn a percentage of all sales they make. However, you must be careful that any scheme does not backfire, by skewing retail sales in favour of products whose sale most benefits staff, rather than the client or salon.

Legislation
Remember that anything you sell must be 'of suitable quality' and 'fit for purpose'.

Checklist: A good selling environment

	Yes	No
Are you smartly and appropriately dressed?	☐	☐
Is the salon clean and tidy?	☐	☐
Do you know the details and costs of the services you sell?	☐	☐
Do you know how to check availability and book an appointment?	☐	☐
Do you know the details and costs of retail products that you sell?	☐	☐
Are all your retail products on display?	☐	☐
Are all your retail products available from stock?	☐	☐
Can you list the promotions you are running at the moment?	☐	☐
Do you know the customer's name?	☐	☐

Customers have a right to a refund under the Supply of Goods and Services Act and you could be in breach of the law if you sell 'dodgy' products. Your professional insurance policy may cover you for sale of products but check the wording as often it limits you to sales to clients only as part of a treatment.

A GOOD SELLING ENVIRONMENT

In order to sell products well, you and the salon in general need to provide a 'good selling environment'.

Many of these points relate to professionalism and competence. Customers will trust in, and buy from, someone who looks smart and professional, knows the products they sell, and can close the sale there and then by having stock or knowing how to make a booking.

IMPROVING YOUR SELLING SKILLS

There are several steps you can take to improve your skills as a salesperson.

• First, address areas of professionalism that you identified as needing

improvement in the checklist above, by looking at the other topics in this book.

• Polish up your product knowledge, on both retail products and services.

• Make sure the client's name is fresh in your mind (and correct) from just before their arrival, to the end of the consultation, when you are booking further consultations, or selling retail products.

'One of the staff just couldn't remember the names of the different conditioners that we sell, no matter how he tried. In the end he asked if I could set up a display near the till, where he could actually see them. This worked great – he didn't have to do it from memory, and it has the added bonus that customers can see the retail products available and often ask to buy some.'

Teri, salon manager

Once you appear professional and know your products, then check to make sure that you are following the basic principles of selling:

Checklist: Selling skills

	Doing it already	Need to improve
Never pre-judge a customer's requirements	☐	☐
Maintain eye contact with the customer	☐	☐
Use good communication skills	☐	☐
Show enthusiasm for products, services and the customer's interests	☐	☐
Identify the customer's needs	☐	☐
Sell a product that suits the customer, not you	☐	☐
Offer a choice, if available	☐	☐
Be positive, but not pushy	☐	☐
Smile, but appear confident, not flippant	☐	☐
Thank the customer	☐	☐

Remember, the aim is that the customer should feel that they have made their own decision, with your support and help. They should feel that they have *chosen to buy* the product or service, not that they having been cajoled or tricked into being *sold* something. In this way, they will be more satisfied and confident in their choice, and more likely to make repeat visits or purchases.

'I was in a local superstore recently. I'd gone in intending to look at DVD players and then buy one, but the salesman just kept pestering me. When I showed an interest in one model, he first of all tried to sell me a much more expensive one bundled with a wide screen TV, then he kept hassling me to make my mind up about buying the other. I felt pressured and that my wishes were being ignored – and I was the one spending the money! In the end I got fed up with being railroaded and left – and I won't go back there in a hurry.'

Iain, centre receptionist

Retail product suppliers often offer some form of training on their products, which may well include simple sales training. You could use these as basic training – the techniques applicable to one retail product can usually be transferred to another.

Also, observe others at work – colleagues, competitors, or sales staff in other retail sectors – and think about which approaches and techniques work best.

END POINTS

- Selling skills will help you to sell retail products or continuing courses of a therapy, to ensure future income.

- Be professional and know your products.

- Provide a good selling environment.

- Help the customer to buy the right products – don't sell them inappropriate ones.

- Customers should feel that they have *chosen to buy* the product or service, not been cajoled or tricked into being *sold* something.

One of the most effective ways of making contact with potential customers is through giving talks and presentations directly to groups of interested people. Talks can focus on your particular therapy or business, what it does (and does not) involve, and its benefits and uses. They give you a very good opportunity to win new customers, either directly or through word of mouth.

'I gave talks at some local coffee mornings about the treatments I offer as a nail technician. I usually demonstrate on whoever is holding the morning, as an incentive. There are usually ten or slightly more people at each, but I have got a couple of regulars out of each morning, and as a result of a recommendation by someone who came to one talk, I did nails for everyone at a big wedding, which was very nice, thank you!'

Jade, nail technician

Unfortunately, presentations, if badly prepared, can make you appear muddled, unprofessional and amateur. However, you can prepare yourself properly by following a few basic principles – none of which are particularly time-consuming or expensive.

PREPARING FOR THE PRESENTATION

Adequate preparation is crucial to the success of a presentation, to help you feel more confident and ensure that your presentation is polished and professional. Bear in mind the three Ws: Why are you doing this? Who is the audience? What is the subject?

'The first couple of times I started again from scratch each time, which took forever and was really daunting. Then I realised that I should keep the same presentation, but just fix the problems and polish the good bits. This means that I have all the stuff ready to go – props, samples, notes, the lot, and really now all I need to do when I am asked to give a presentation is check that it's all there and read through the notes to remind myself.'

James, aromatherapist

Checklist: Thinking through a presentation

Have you clearly established the purpose of the presentation?	☐
Do you know what the audience expect to hear?	☐
Do you know what benefits the audience will expect to get from the presentation?	☐
Have you decided why you are giving the presentation?	☐
Have you selected and ordered what to say?	☐
Have you decided on the level of what you will say?	☐
Do you know what demonstrations and props are needed or appropriate?	☐

Why are you doing this?

Begin by making sure that you are clear about why you are doing the presentation – is it to increase sales, publicise a new venture or salon, or to broaden public awareness of your discipline? Or is it all of these?

You can use this checklist when you are preparing a presentation to help you clarify some of the basics.

Who is the audience?

'I took along lots of equipment to show off: massage bench, OHTs and all. The audience turned out to be just six people, so actually I just grouped them around in a circle and turned the talk into a more informal and friendly question-and-answer session, which in the end worked out well.'

Bryan, masseur

Checklist: Know your audience

Do you know how many people will be in the audience?	☐
Are they going to be experts or novices?	☐
Will they be interested in particular areas of the subject?	☐
Are they likely to be already convinced about the topic?	☐
Will they be young or old, rich or poor, male or female?	☐

It is important to take into account the size and make-up of your audience, in order to pitch your presentation appropriately, and use the right aids and/or handouts.

Checklist: Getting the subject matter right

Can you make the topic interesting and stimulating?	☐
Is the topic appropriate for the audience?	☐
Can you cover the topic in the time available?	☐
Do you know what you are talking about?	☐
Will the topic be understood by the audience?	☐
Are you up to date on the subject?	☐

What is the subject?

Think about the topic and try to shape what you are going to say about it to match the audience you expect, and to fulfil your reasons for giving the presentation.

THE STRUCTURE OF THE PRESENTATION

Your presentation should have three distinct stages:

1 introduction

2 development

3 conclusion.

At the end of the presentation you should allow time for questions.

Introduction

The first few sentences of a presentation greatly affect how the audience responds to the rest, and hence its success or failure. Make an impact; whet the audience's

Checklist: What to do in an introduction

Welcome your audience and introduce yourself.	☐
State the topic, length and purpose of the presentation (and recap earlier presentations if it is part of a series).	☐
Outline what you are going to say.	☐
Explain how the audience can participate.	☐
Cover housekeeping issues such as loos, fire exits, etc.	☐
Tell the audience when you will take questions.	☐

appetite by arousing their interest and curiosity. Be enthusiastic, positive and possibly slightly provocative. The checklist on the following page gives some ideas about things to cover in an introduction.

Development

This is the main body of the talk where you will discuss your theme or make your demonstrations. It is important that you plan carefully to link the elements of your talk together, perhaps around a visual aid. For example, if you are talking about the use of a massage bench, then plan to describe the adjustments and features in sequence from one end to the other, rather than hopping around.

Depending on your needs, there are different ways of structuring your presentation.

If you don't have much time

Put the big idea up front – state your idea, then back it up, but be careful of using this approach if the audience may be antagonistic or sceptical.

If you want to persuade

Build up to it – start with background information, develop the issues, reveal your rationale and come to the big idea. Lead the audience on a journey. This is good if the audience is sceptical or uninformed on the topic, but takes time and may cause information overload.

If you want to give information

When the primary objective is to provide information for the audience, a good structure is essential for them to assimilate the information. It can help to summarise the structure using visual aids (e.g. a flip chart) and/or audience notes (e.g. a handout). You can:

- use a cause-and-effect approach – discuss the cause before the effect

- take a chronological order approach – especially if you are describing the development of a technique or therapy

- move from the easy to the hard – build up to the complex issues

- break the issue down into separate parts and deal with each separately.

Conclusion

The conclusion is the time to reinforce the message of your presentation. Conclude your talk by briefly summarising your main points. You should:

- emphasise the key arguments (and review your objectives if appropriate)

- never introduce new material in the conclusion

- tell the audience about future events (if any)

- thank your audience.

Questions

Don't take questions during the talk. Plan to take them at the end, or at natural breaks in the talk. Explain at the start when you will take questions.

PREPARE NOTES

Prepare a sequence of cards that contain the main points of your talk. One should be enough for the introduction, the development may need several, and the conclusion should need just one again. Identify on the cards what you should do and what props you need.

Don't write down an entire speech to read out. This will be boring and lose the attention of your audience within minutes.

Cards

'The first time I used cards to help give a talk, I just wrote things out on lots of sheets of A4 paper, and forgot to number them. They were too big and floppy to hold so I had to put them down on a desk and pick them up one at a time as I needed them. This really broke up my flow and made me very nervous. To cap it all someone came in late and the draft when he opened the door blew all of the notes onto the floor. It took ages to work out the right order. I was mortified.'

Karen, homeopath

The important thing about your cards is that they should:

• be clear and concise

• be easy to read

• be easy to handle, and numbered (you could drop them!)

• use key words and phrases.

A card could look like this:

Card no 1

Theme: Massage and Mars

Introduction:

→ Long flights to Mars

→ Muscle wastage

→ Massage to the rescue!

Props and visual aids

Make sure that the equipment, treatment benches, towels, samples or other props and visual aids that you need are available and working. If you are using a colleague as a model subject, practise with them. A picture is worth a thousand words, and a demonstration even more than that. Visual aids can:

• add structure to the presentation

• help demonstrate difficult concepts

• provide you with an aide-mémoire

• help with recapping

• immediately communicate treatments and procedures

• hold an audience's interest.

'Our receptionist had come along to be a subject, but had worn a long narrow skirt which meant she had problems getting onto the massage bench.'

Michael, owner of natural therapy centre

END POINTS

In this topic we have looked at how to prepare a successful presentation. Remember the three Ws of preparing good presentations.

• **Why** are you doing the presentation; what do you hope to achieve by it?

• **Who** is your audience? Your talk must be appropriate for them.

• **What** is your talk about? You must present your topic as well as you can, bearing in mind the previous two points.

The last topic looked at how you can prepare the structure and content of any presentation you give. Presentations can be very useful to spread the word about your therapy or profession. You could present the value of, say, aromatherapy, to groups of employers, sports experts, nurses or general practitioners. Look around to see where such groups meet and offer to make a presentation. You will also need to make practical preparations, such as making sure you have the right equipment and notes, and setting up the room properly beforehand to give you the best chance of being able to deliver a good, entertaining presentation. Very few people can carry off a successful presentation that has had little or no proper preparation.

This topic looks at these further preparations, as well as some of the skills of presentation, such as speaking.

PRACTICAL PRESENTING

If you are well prepared then, if you get the practicalities right, your presentation will be more relaxed, professional and effective.

Rehearse

If you can rehearse in the room where you will deliver the presentation, great. If not, anywhere will do as long as you do rehearse. The key to giving a successful talk or demonstration is *practice*.

Rehearse in front of friends or colleagues, or record yourself on a tape recorder or video camera and play it back – this can be very revealing, and gives you a good chance to check that the pace and length of presentation is right.

'My brother-in-law bought a video camera, so I borrowed it and filmed myself giving my talk. When I watched it I realised that I just kept fiddling with my glasses – pushing them back up my nose all the time, so my hand was always in front of my face and mouth. Since then, I've always worn my contact lenses when giving a talk.'

Stephen, aromatherapist

Arrange the room

Arrive in plenty of time to arrange the room to suit you. Try to ensure that there are no barriers, such as large desks, between you and the audience, and encourage them to sit at the front. Welcome them as they arrive and try to judge their mood.

'If there are too many chairs, people always sit as far back as possible, leaving loads of empty ones at the front. I always stack a lot of the chairs at the sides of the room so that people have to come and sit close – if there aren't enough chairs out, they can always put a few back out.'

Mia, colour therapist

Have the right props and visual aids

Make sure also that all the equipment, treatment benches, towels, samples or other props and visual aids that you need are available and working. If you are using a colleague as a model subject, ensure that they turn up before the audience.

Make sure also, that you have your:

- appointment book
- sample products
- product information leaflets
- treatment information leaflets
- price lists.

Use your notes

Your notes provide the framework for your presentation. They will also give you confidence, so whatever you do, make sure that you remember to bring them with you and use them.

Use bullet points to help you remember your points, rather than reading from your notes.

Before the audience arrives, run through the cards in order to refresh your memory of the structure of the presentation. The notes on the cards will remind you of the content as you are giving the talk.

'I now make a sort of index card which I don't use in the talk, but it goes at the front of the pile and lists the other cards. It helps me remember what the sequence is without going through all the cards.'

Tony, Reiki master

Use humour

Humour can help break the ice, maintain attention and enliven a presentation, but you must use it carefully, and it must be appropriate to your audience. Don't be sarcastic, and don't overdo it – you're a therapist not a comedian.

'I try to start with a joke. If people are still settling down and there's a bit of noise, I speak up and use the joke to make them

laugh. This brings their attention back to me and I can start the talk proper with them already focussed on what I'm saying.'

Larissa, Indian head masseuse

Speak confidently and professionally

If you want to get some tips on how professionals use gestures and expression in presentations, watch the presenters of TV shows. Observe their gestures, listen to the tone and pace of their voices, and see how they manage to involve you, even from the other side of a camera.

Speaking well

When giving a presentation:

- identify the aim and objectives of the session. If you can negotiate content with the audience, the talk will be that much more applicable to them
- speak clearly, audibly and as naturally as you can – don't worry about an accent if your speech is clear
- vary the pitch, volume and intonation of your voice, and use pauses for emphasis
- maintain a steady speed – most people speak more quickly when nervous. Rehearse to get the right pace and timing
- maintain eye contact, looking at all the audience – this will help to involve the audience in a two-way communication. The aim is to talk *with* your audience not *at* them
- be careful of poor non-verbal communication such as crossed arms, but don't be lifeless – use gesture (within reason) to emphasise your points
- avoid bad grammar
- always have a little extra something to say – a story or anecdote or something about your particular interests – in case you finish early and have some time to fill.

We all get nervous before and during presentations, and we all have our own mannerisms. To avoid distracting the audience from the content of the presentation you should:

- stand still – don't prowl to and fro

- relax, but don't slouch

- remove any coins or keys from your pockets so that you can't play with them without realising.

Deal with the unexpected

Sometimes interruptions occur – unexpected noises such as road drills, car alarms, ice cream vans, noisy aircraft, etc. Some of the audience may arrive late or leave early. At worst, you may have to evacuate the room because of a fire alarm.

- Remember that it is your presentation, and stay in control. Apologise to the audience and pause until the distraction passes.

- Never show anger towards late arrivals – you don't know why they are late.

- If someone is talking loudly and distracting you, then first show interest by looking at them. If this doesn't work, pause your talk and look at them – this often embarrasses people into silence. If this doesn't work, pause and explain to them that you are finding it hard to continue whilst they are interrupting.

Answering questions

When dealing with questions:

- be pleased – they show the audience is involved and what they want to know

- repeat the question before answering it so that the whole audience can hear

- deal with them equally or you will lose credibility

- give brief answers so you can take more questions

- don't bluff – if you don't know the answer say so, but offer to respond later

- never ridicule a question, as you will rapidly antagonise the audience

- warn when time is running out, e.g. 'Time for another two questions only'.

Make sure that you take any orders and make any bookings that are requested.

AFTERWARDS

Try to learn from each presentation that you give. Make a note of things that went wrong, things that went really well, and audience questions, and adjust the presentation in the light of these. Follow up any queries, questions or leads that you received from the audience during the presentation within a couple of days.

END POINTS

In this topic we have looked at practical ways to ensure the success of any presentation you have to give – planning is the key to success.

Think of giving good presentations as the four Ps.

- **Plan** ahead, so that you know what you are going to do and say, and what you will need.

- **Prepare** your props, aids, assistant, the room, your notes.

- **Practise** your speaking and delivery.

- **Polish** your performance by learning from each presentation and improving accordingly.

Section 5

Resources

Topic	Page

If you are interested in finding out more about a particular topic that has been covered in this book (or perhaps one that hasn't), this section contains suggestions of things that will help you.

1. ITEC Code of Practice

The ITEC Code of Practice is provided as an example of a professional code of practice.

2. Sample forms and letters

We have included a collection of sample letters and forms that you might find helpful in the early days of your business.

3. Books, websites, addresses and other resources

No one book will contain everything you need to know about setting up a business, but we hope this one has provided a good basis. We have also included a list of books, magazines, journals and websites that have more detail on specific aspects of setting up and running your business.

There is also a list of addresses and websites where you may be able to find information about particular aspects of working as a therapist or setting up in business.

1. ITEC REGISTERED THERAPISTS' CODE OF PRACTICE

1. ITEC professionals shall only offer to treat, and/or treat, clients within their own trained professional competence and shall not practise any therapy or treatment for which they are not properly qualified.

2. ITEC professionals will not treat any person or give any advice to any person on or relating to treatments for which they do not hold professional indemnity insurance cover.

3. ITEC professionals shall at all times act in a professional, ethical and honourable manner towards their clients and members of public. Client modesty shall be maintained at all times.

4. ITEC professionals shall at all times keep entirely confidential between themselves and their clients all matters relating to consultations, treatment, advice and clinical matters other than with the consent of the client or when reporting treatments or clinical findings to a fellow professional or medical advisor.

5. ITEC professionals shall keep, and maintain in a secure place, clinical records of all treatments and consultations for each client and shall do so under the terms of the current law of their country as regards Data Protection legislation.

6. ITEC professionals will not promote themselves other than in a responsible and honest manner that does not bring themselves, ITEC, ITEC professionals or the treatments that they are offering into any form of disrepute. Further, they will make no claim for potential success in any treatment that cannot be fully authenticated by ITEC professionals and/or validated research.

7. Where an ITEC professional is working under the direction of a medical practitioner, the ITEC professional will not undertake any treatments or procedures other than those prescribed in writing by the medical practitioner and will always defer to the clinical judgement and direction of the medical practitioner and will not seek to undermine or advise against any treatment prescribed.

8. Where an ITEC professional is working within any form of hospital she/he will always follow the procedures of the establishment and will at no time undertake treatment or offer to undertake treatment other than under the direction and approval of the

medical staff of the establishment. Further, they will at no time imply that they are members of staff of the establishment unless that is the case.

9 Where an ITEC professional believes that a client may have a condition that could require medical treatment or treatment by a therapist in a different discipline she/he must cease treatment and recommend that the client contact the appropriate professional for a diagnosis.

10. The ITEC professional must at all times make her/himself aware of the notifiable diseases that are listed for the local area. Where a client presents with any notifiable disease, the ITEC professional must insist that the client contact her/his medical practitioner and record the statement in the client notes.

11. Children (persons under 16 years of age) may not be treated without the personal or written permission of the child's parent or legal guardian.

12. ITEC professionals will not, when treating a client who has been referred to her/him by another therapist, seek to attract that client as their own direct client without the permission of the other therapist.

13. Any ITEC professional who is employed or contracted to a salon, clinic or other organisation or individual shall not seek to attract, unless permitted by the proprietor, as her/his own clients, any client of that organisation or individual who was treated by that salon, clinic, organisation or individual.

14. Where an ITEC professional is formally charged with any criminal offence that in the opinion of the ITEC Professionals Council is such that the ITEC professional's reputation as a therapist is in jeopardy, the Council may suspend that ITEC professional's registration pending the outcome of any proceedings.

15. ITEC professionals may designate themselves as 'Mem. ITEC Professionals' and use the suffix 'Dip. (or Cert.) ITEC' plus the treatment, e.g. 'Dip. ITEC Aroma' after their names.

16. ITEC professionals must provide evidence that they are covered by indemnity insurance for both their treatments and the products that they may use and/or sell to clients, sufficient for the levels of compensation likely to be required in the country in which they work. For UK and Ireland the level of cover should be at a minimum of £1,000,000.

Copyright ITEC 2000

2. SAMPLE FORMS AND LETTERS

The following documents are included here:

Business plan executive summary

Sample job description

Sample person specification

ITEC client record card

Cancellation notice

Continuing professional development (CPD) record card

Accident record card

Patient GP contact consent form

Consent to treatment form

Letter of introduction to a GP

Sample job advertisement

Contract of employment

BUSINESS PLAN EXECUTIVE SUMMARY   20ᵀᴴ JUNE 2002

Lissia Charolet-Davies, Alexander Technique teacher

Mission statement	To provide home- and office-based training in the Alexander Technique.
Products and services	The services offered will be 45-minute Alexander Technique training sessions.
Work location	In the client's own home or office, within an approximate radius of fifteen miles from Cambridge, i.e. Newmarket, Huntingdon, Ely, etc. Sessions will be grouped by day to reduce travelling costs – i.e. Huntingdon one day, Cambridge the next, etc.
Unique selling points	Home- and office-based training in the Alexander Technique, which is: • convenient for the client because they don't have to travel • convenient for the client because it is arranged at a time to suit them • delivered in an environment in which the client is at ease – their own home or office • cost-effective because of reduced overheads.
Client base	Singers, musicians, dancers and athletes, who wish to explore their full performing potential. Sufferers of RSI, carpal tunnel syndrome, chronic back pain or postural problems.
Estimated product prices	£30 per 45-minute session.
Estimated product costs	The technique requires no consumables. The main costs will be travel costs to clients' premises. At 35p per mile and assuming an average journey of 10 miles, this equals £3.50 per visit.
Estimated sales volume	Based on previous experience I expect to fill 75% of my eight daily one-hour slots (45 minutes treatment plus 15 minutes travel). This represents 30 sessions per week, and approx 1300 sessions per year (making allowance for sickness, statutory and other holidays).
Income versus expenditure	1300 sessions per year equates to an income of £39,000 per year. Expenditure on this will be £4,550 in travel costs, plus fixed costs of £1,100 per year, made up of professional fees, indemnity insurance, advertising costs, and depreciation costs of a treatment bench (straight-line over four years). This leaves a pre-tax income of £33,350.

SAMPLE JOB DESCRIPTION

Job title:

Receptionist/Administrative Assistant

Responsible to:

Centre Manager

Main purpose of job:

to staff the reception area, take calls and bookings, perform general administrative duties as required.

Duties include:

- answering the telephone
- booking appointments for therapies
- writing and despatching routine or straightforward letters
- sorting and opening post
- obtaining information from the computer
- maintaining records, filing systems and computer files
- ordering stationery.

Role:

As Receptionist you will be the first contact that most clients and suppliers have with the centre. You will have to take bookings and maintain the appointment books efficiently. Administrative duties (stock ordering, mail processing, etc.) will have to be carried out so that the centre runs smoothly and efficiently.

The centre is aiming to move its appointment system, client and stock records onto a computer, and you may have to undertake necessary computer training.

Goals:

- to create a professional, courteous and presentable image of the centre.
- to ensure availability of stock at all times.
- to become proficient in the use of the new computer system.

Targets:

- to answer all incoming calls within three rings.
- to order replacement stock items within one day of stock levels reaching re-order point.

Salaries and benefits:

- the starting salary will be £12,000 per annum.
- holiday entitlement is 20 days paid at normal rate after first year of service.

CANCELLATION NOTICE

Pilgrim Holistic Therapies are delighted to assist our clients by reserving treatment time in advance or booking courses of treatments.

Please note, however, that we will charge for treatments booked in advance and cancelled at less than 24 hours' notice.

SAMPLE PERSON SPECIFICATION

Criteria	Essential	Desirable	How assessed
1. Skills/Abilities	Keyboard skills Efficient, methodical	Ability to use fax machines and photocopiers Computer literate	Application form (A/F), test
2. Knowledge	Knowledge of appointment booking systems	Knowledge of complementary therapies	A/F, interview
3. Qualifications/ Education/Training	Two GCSEs (grade C or above) or equivalent including English	Undertaken training in computer software packages such as Windows	A/F, exercise, test
4. Experience	1 year's receptionist experience	Record-keeping, stock control. Experience in complementary therapy environment	A/F, interview
5. Personal qualities	Presentable, good interpersonal skills		Interview
6. Other requirements		Current UK driving licence	A/F

CONTINUING PROFESSIONAL DEVELOPMENT (CPD) RECORD CARD

Use this card to keep a record of the activities that contribute towards your continuing professional development over the year. Courses and other training count, but activities like keeping up to date by reading professional journals each month are also valuable components of CPD, as is time spent studying on your own.

Name: _____   Year: _____

Date	CPD activity description	Hours
	Total hours:	

I confirm that this record card represents my CPD activities for the year.

Signed: _____   Date: _____

MASSAGE CLIENT RECORD CARD

Client's name: _____   Date: _____

Address: _____   Sex: Male ❏ Female ❏

_____   Date of birth: _____

_____   Height: _____

Tel No: Day: _____ Eve: _____   Weight: _____

GP Address: _____   Profession: _____

Marital status: Single ❏ Married ❏ Separated ❏ Divorced ❏ Widowed ❏

No. & Age of Children/Dependants: _____

Pregnant: No ❏ Yes ❏ How many months? _____

Parental history: _____
_____

Medical history/Operations: _____
_____

Medication/Present health: _____
_____

Reason for treatment: _____
_____

Muscular/Skeletal problems: Neck ❏ Back ❏ Rheumatism ❏ Aches & Pains ❏ Stiff joints ❏ Headaches ❏

Digestive problems: Constipation ❏ Bloating ❏ Liver/gall bladder ❏ Stomach ❏

Circulation: Heart ❏ Blood pressure ❏ Fluid retention ❏ Tired legs ❏ Varicose veins ❏ Cellulite ❏

Kidney problems ❏ Cold hands and feet

Gynaecological: Irregular periods ❏ P.M.T ❏ Menopause ❏ H.R.T ❏ Pill ❏ Coil ❏ Other _____

Nervous system: Sensitive ❏ Migraine ❏ Tension ❏ Headaches ❏ Stress ❏ Depression ❏

Immune system: Prone to infections ❏ Sore throats ❏ Colds ❏ Chest ❏ Sinuses ❏

Regular antibiotic taken ❏

Professional life (Job details): _____

Ability to relax: Good ❏ Poor ❏ Average ❏

Time for Self: Hobbies or Creative Interests: _____

Sleep patterns: Good ❏ Poor ❏ Average no. of hours ❏

Do you see daylight in your workplace? Yes ❏ No ❏

Do you suffer from: Nervous tension ❏ Depression ❏ Anxiety ❏

Do you eat regular meals? Yes ❏ No ❏

Do you eat in a hurry? Yes ❏ No ❏

Do you take food/vitamin supplements? Yes ❏ No ❏

Do you exercise? Yes ❏ No ❏

Is your diet well balanced? Yes ❏ No ❏ _____

How much of each of these items does your diet contain:

Fresh fruit: _____

Fresh vegetables: _____

Protein (source?): _____

Dairy produce:_____

Sweet things? _____

Added salt: _____   Added sugar: _____

How many daily drinks of tea:_____   Coffee: _____

Fruit Juices: _____   Water: _____

Soft Drinks:_____   Other:_____

Do you suffer from food allergies? Yes ❑ No ❑ Bingeing: Yes ❑ No ❑ Overeating: Yes ❑ No ❑

Do you smoke? No ❑ Yes ❑ How many per day? __

Do you drink? No ❑ Light ❑ Medium ❑ Heavy ❑ Units per week:_____

Do you exercise? None ❑ Occasional ❑ Irregular ❑ Regular ❑ Types: _____

What is your skin type: Dry ❑ Oily ❑ Combination ❑ Sensitive ❑ Dehydrated ❑

Do you suffer from: Dermatitis: Yes ❑ No ❑ Acne: Yes ❑ No ❑ Eczema: Yes ❑ No ❑

Psoriasis: Yes ❑ No ❑ Allergies: Yes ❑ No ❑ Hay Fever: Yes ❑ No ❑ Asthma: Yes ❑ No ❑

Signature: _____

Date: _____

Treatment results

Treatment 1

Date: _____

Treatment 2

Date: _____

Treatment 3

Date: _____

Treatment 4

Date: _____

Accident record sheet

Pilgrim Holistic Therapies, Elver Lane, Landbeach CB0 0XX

Date	Time	What happened and where	Action taken	Confirmed as accurate	
				Pilgrim	Client
22/05/2003	10.45 am	Mr Sumner (who was wearing sandals) pricked his right big toe on a thorn in the driveway to the centre	Provided a plaster. Advised Mr Sumner to see his GP re: the state of his Tetanus immunisation	M Smallwell	A E Sumner

PATIENT GP CONTACT CONSENT FORM

Pilgrim Holistic Therapies

I agree that any relevant notes or comments from my General Practitioner may be sent to:

Michael Smallroch

Pilgrim Holistic Therapies

Elver Lane

Landbeach

CB0 0XX

Signed: *A E Sumner*

Name (capitals): ALBERT EDWARD SUMNER

Address: Stanley Cottage, Mill Lane, Yateley, Hants

Date: 16/4/2003

CONSENT TO TREATMENT FORM

Pilgrim Holistic Therapies

I consent to receiving _____ treatment, having been informed about the nature of the treatment and any possible side effects.

Name

Signature

Date

LETTER OF INTRODUCTION TO A GP

Pilgrim Holistic Therapies
Elver Lane
Landbeach
CB0 0XX

Dear Dr Hardy

I am writing to let you know that we have recently added the Alexander Technique to the therapies available at the centre. This is a personal pleasure for me, as I myself experienced great benefits from the Alexander Technique in treating the stresses and pains I suffered in my previous career in Marketing.

You may know that Alexander Technique involves learning to use the body in the most efficient way. It is widely taught in music and drama colleges to enhance a performer's co-ordination, and has applications as diverse as sport and pregnancy. It aims to:

• reduce pain and stiffness

• increase mobility

• teach people to stand, sit and move 'correctly'

• reduce back and other posture-related problems

• improve grace and co-ordination.

The Technique does not seek to 'treat' specific ailments but to realise the considerable therapeutic benefits of changing harmful habits.

It is based on the principle that we function as a whole and, to effect beneficial change, we must learn consciously to prevent unwanted, unnecessary and harmful habits (such as reacting too quickly to stimuli, unduly stiffening and tightening muscles and joints, and putting too much effort and tension into activities). Becoming aware of what we are actually doing is part of the process of learning and applying the Alexander Technique.

The Alexander Technique has been the subject of several scientific studies and its effectiveness is well documented. Doctors and consultants now recommend it more frequently, and many medical insurance companies now pay for treatments.

Our new therapist, Mme Lissia Charolet-Davies, trained at [[XYZ College]] and is a member of [[Professional Organisation]].

I enclose information sheets on all therapies available at the centre. If you feel that any of your patients might benefit from the Alexander Technique, or any of our other complementary therapies, please contact us.

Yours truly
M Smallroch
Michael Smallroch

SAMPLE JOB ADVERTISEMENT

Pilgrim Holistic Therapies, a busy clinic offering a variety of therapies, requires a Receptionist/Administrative Assistant to work in its centre near Cambridge.

The successful candidate will enjoy working as part of a dedicated team, with the added satisfaction of working for a clinic committed to providing professionally delivered and client-centred therapies.

The job involves manning our busy reception area, welcoming clients and creating a professional and welcoming impression, together with a variety of administrative duties. These will include appointment booking and record keeping, filing, letter writing, sorting post, and ordering stock. Training will be provided, if necessary, to equip the job holder with computer skills to enable them to use the centre's computer system.

Applicants are required to have 2 GCSEs at grade C or above (or equivalent), including English Language, and preferably some experience in administration. An interest in, and empathy with, complementary therapies would be an advantage.

Salary will start at £12,000.

Holiday entitlement of 20 days per annum after first year of service.

Please write for an application form to:
Michael Smallroch
Pilgrim Holistic Therapies
Elver Lane
Landbeach
CB0 0XX

For further information contact Michael Smallroch on: 01223 462023

Closing date for applications : 19th August 2003

Interview Date: 4th September 2003

Pilgrim Holistic Therapies is an equal opportunities employer, and welcomes applications from all sections of the community.

CONTRACT OF EMPLOYMENT

Dated:

BETWEEN

(1) xxxxx ("the Employer")

(2) xxxxx ("the Employee")

Our agreement with you:

IT IS AGREED that the Employer will employ the Employee on the following terms and conditions:

1. Terms of Employment

1.1 The Employee is employed to work at the Employer's premises at xxxxx or such other place(s) as the Employer may reasonably require from time to time. The employment commences on xxxxx and shall not be continuous with any previous period of employment.

1.2 The Employee's job title shall be xxxxx. The Employee's duties shall be:

(a) xxxxx

(b) xxxxx

(c) xxxxx

(d) xxxxx

(e) xxxxx

1.3 The Employee shall normally work the following days: xxxxx

1.4 Normal working hours shall be agreed by the Employer and Employee in advance, but shall generally be xxxxx.

1.5 The Employee shall be entitled to a rest period of not less than 11 consecutive hours between the end of her normal working hours on one day and the commencement of her normal working hours on the following day. It shall be the responsibility of the Employee to ensure that she takes such a rest period.

1.6 Unless prevented by illness or injury the Employee:

(a) shall devote the whole of her time, attention and ability, both during normal working hours and during such other reasonable additional hours as may be agreed between the Employer and Employee, for the performance of her duties for the employer, and

(b) follow all lawful instructions of the Employer,

(c) not perform any paid or unpaid work for any third party without the prior written consent of the Employer.

2. Remuneration

2.1 The Employee's gross salary will be £ xxxxx per (week/month). The salary shall be reviewed (once/twice) a year but any increase in salary shall be at the total discretion of the Employer.

2.2 The salary shall be payable in arrears on the last working day in each (week/month) by a cheque or a direct debit payment direct to the Employee's bank, as agreed by the parties. The Employer shall ensure that the Employee is given a payslip on the date of payment detailing gross payment, deductions and net payment.

2.3 The Employee shall receive the following benefits:

(a) Accommodation

The Employer provides the following accommodation:

(b) Meals

The Employer provides the following meals:

(c) Use of car

The Employer (does/does not) provide the use of a car.

(d) Pension

The Employer (does/does not) provide pension contributions.

(e) Private Health Insurance

The Employer (does/does not) provide private health insurance.

2.4 The Employee shall be reimbursed by the Employer for all reasonable expenses incurred by her in the performance of her duties under this contract, provided that the expenses are incurred with the approval of the

Employer and provided the Employee produces such evidence of expenditure as the Employer may reasonably require. Petrol costs will be reimbursed at the rate recommended by the Automobile Association if the Employee uses her own car during performance of her duties.

2.5 The Employee agrees that the Employer shall be entitled to deduct from any amount payable to the Employee under this contract:

(a) any deductions required by law (including PAYE income tax, and National Insurance contributions), and

(b) any monies owed by her to the Employer by way of reimbursement.

2.6 The Employer shall be responsible for accounting to the Inland Revenue for income tax and the Employer's and the Employee's National Insurance Contributions.

3. Holidays

3.1 The holiday year will start on xxxx.

3.2 In each holiday year the Employee's holiday entitlement is xx days in addition to the usual public holidays/ The Employee shall not be entitled to paid time off for public and bank holidays except with the express agreement of the Employer.

3.3 Holiday pay will be made at the Employee's normal rate of remuneration. One day's accrued holiday pay is equivalent to 1/260th of the Employee's salary.

3.4 The Employee will not be allowed to carry holiday forward from one leave year to the next or (subject to clause 3.7) receive payment in lieu of any untaken holiday entitlement, and the Employee shall ensure that she takes such entitlement within the holiday year.

3.5 The Employee shall give the Employer not less than xxxxx notice of an intention to take holiday. If the holiday period requested is not convenient to the Employer, the Employer shall agree an alternative period, which is convenient to both parties. The Employee will not be allowed to take more than 10 working days holiday at any one time. There is no entitlement to take unpaid holidays. (Please note this clause must not be used if it effectively deprives the Employee of taking her holiday in the holiday year.)

3.6 Where the Employee is working out any notice following either party giving notice to terminate this contract, the Employee may be required to take any unused holiday during that notice period.

3.7 On the termination of her employment, the Employee will be paid any holiday entitlement accrued but not taken. If the Employee has taken more days holiday than her accrued entitlement, the Employer will make the appropriate deduction from the Employee's final salary payment (calculated in accordance with Clause 3.3).

3.8 If the Employee is required to work on a bank or other public holiday, the Employee will be given a day off in lieu on a date to be agreed by the Employer.

4. Sickness & Sick Pay

4.1 If the Employee is unable to attend work due to sickness or injury she shall (insofar as she is able) promptly notify the Employer either in person or by telephone (as appropriate) on the first day of absence and provide the Employer with such evidence of her sickness or injury and the cause of it as the Employer may from time to time reasonably require.

4.2 The Employee shall be entitled to receive either Statutory Sick Pay in accordance with the Government SSP scheme during periods of sickness absence, or payment [inclusive of any Statutory Sick Pay] during her absence on sick leave in accordance with the following:

(a) Full pay for the first (xxxxx) days/weeks sick-leave

(b) Half pay for (xxxxx) days/weeks and

(c) thereafter, Statutory Sick Pay in accordance with the Government's SSP scheme.

4.3 The Employer shall be entitled to require the Employee to undergo examinations by a medical practitioner appointed by the Employer, and the Employee shall sign the necessary consent form to authorize the medical practitioner to disclose to the Employer the results of the examination and discuss with the employer any matters arising from the examination that might impair the Employee's ability to discharge her duties properly.

4.4 If the Employee takes sick leave due to injuries caused to her by a third party, and the Employee recovers damages from the third party for her injuries, the damages recovered shall include all payments made to the Employee by the Employer during the sick leave and all payments recovered shall then be paid to the Employer as soon as possible.

5. Confidentiality

5.1 The Employee shall not during her employment with the Employer, or at any time thereafter (otherwise than in the proper course of her duties or as is required by law) without the prior written approval of the Employer, divulge or disclose any information which, by reason of its character or the circumstances or manner of its disclosure, is evidently confidential to the Employer or to the Employer's clients.

6. Termination

6.1 If either party wishes to terminate this contract, the notice to be given shall be as follows:

(a) during the first four weeks of employment ("the Probationary Period"), not less than xxxxx

(b) thereafter, not less than xxxxx weeks notice in writing. The notice shall never be less than the statutory minimum period of one week until the Employee has completed two years' continuous employment, and thereafter one additional week's notice for every full year of continuous employment up to a maximum of twelve weeks.

6.2 The Employee's employment under this contract may be terminated by the Employer at any time immediately and without any notice or payment in lieu of notice if the Employee:

(a) is guilty of gross misconduct or serious and persistent breaches of the terms of this contract, or

(b) is convicted of any criminal offence involving dishonesty, violence, causing death or personal injury, or damaging property.

6.3 Misconduct that may be deemed gross misconduct includes but is not limited to theft, drunkenness, illegal drug taking, child abuse, and violent or threatening behaviour (be it verbal or physical).

7. Disciplinary & Capability Procedure

7.1 Reasons which might give rise to the need for measures under the Disciplinary & Capability Procedure include the following:

(a) causing a disruptive influence in the workplace

(b) job incompetence

(c) unsatisfactory standard of dress or appearance

(d) conduct inside or outside normal working hours prejudicial to the interests or reputation of the Employer

(e) unreliability in timekeeping or attendance

(f) failure to comply with instructions and procedures

(g) loss of driving licence

(h) breach of confidentiality.

7.2 In the event of the Employer needing to take disciplinary action the procedure shall, save in cases involving gross misconduct, be:

Firstly: verbal warning

Secondly: written warning

Thirdly: dismissal.

8. Grievance Procedure

If the Employee has any reasonable grievance relating to her employment, the matter should be raised with the Employer either in person or in writing as the Employee deems appropriate. The Employer and the Employee agree to take all such reasonable steps as are necessary to resolve such grievances.

9. General

9.1 This contract shall be construed in accordance with and governed by the laws of England and Wales/Scotland/Northern Ireland and the parties submit to the exclusive jurisdiction of the Courts of England and Wales/Scotland/Northern Ireland.

9.2 Any reference in this contract to any statutory provision shall be deemed to include a reference to any statutory modification or re-enactment of it and shall also include reference to all statutory instruments and orders made pursuant to any such statutory provision.

9.3 Words in the singular shall include the plural and vice versa, and references to any gender shall include the other and a reference to a person shall include a reference to any Company as well as any legal or natural person.

SIGNED by the Employer
DATED

SIGNED by the Employee
DATED

3. BOOKS, WEBSITES, ADDRESSES AND OTHER RESOURCES

Section 1 Setting up and running the business

Several of the books listed for this section have useful information relating to other sections as well.

Companies House publish a number of free guides that can be found at www.companieshouse.gov.uk

Brown, R and Barrow, C (2001) *The Business Plan Workbook* 4th edition. Kogan Paul: London

Greener, M (1987) *Penguin Business Dictionary* Penguin

Harland, N and Finn, G (1995) *Healthy Business: The Natural Practitioner's Guide to Success* 4th edition. Hyden House Ltd: Clanfield, Hampshire

Hingston, P and Balfour, A (2001) *Working from Home* Dorling Kindersley

Hussey, R (ed.) (1999) *The Oxford Dictionary of Accounting* Oxford University Press

Jones, G (1999) *How to Start a Business from Home* 4th edition. How to Books: Oxford

Keenan, D and Riches, S (2001) *Business Law* 6th edition. Longman

McMahon, G (1994) *Setting up your own Private Practice in Counselling and Psychotherapy* National Extension College: Cambridge

Stone, P (2001) *Financing a New Business* How to books: Oxford

Whitely, J (2002) *Be Your Own Boss* How to Books: Oxford

Williams, D (1994) *Running Your Own Business* Nicholas Brearley Publishing Ltd

Williams, S (2001) *Small Business Guide* 15th edition. Press Vitess: London

www.startups.co.uk is a helpful website containing articles, books, and frequently updated guidance on setting up in business.

www.dti.gov.uk is a useful site about trade and industry, including employment rights.

www.hse.gov.uk is the Health and Safety Executive's website. You can also contact them on 08701 545500 to find out the address of your local office.

www.open.gov.uk is a general law site giving information about court service and recent legislation.

www.sfedi.co.uk is the website for the Small Firms Enterprise Development Initiative. You can also contact them on 0114 209 6269.

www.managementandleadershipcouncil.org is the website for The Council for Excellence in Management and Leadership. It contains publications and resources, including a Business Improvement Tool, which can help you to identify the strengths and weaknesses in your business.

Section 2 Relationships, professionalism and ethics

Cook, S (2002) *Customer Care* Kogan Page

Covey, S (1989) *The 7 Habits of Highly Effective People* Simon and Schuster

Rigazzi-Tarling, I (2000) *Creating an Excellent Salon* Hodder and Stoughton

Roberts, E and Williams, J (1997) *Warning Signs and Similar Symptoms: A Desktop Reference Guide for Alternative and Complementary Practitioners* Winter Press

Wellemin, J (1998) *Successful Customer Care in a Week* Hodder and Stoughton

Codes of Practice

The ITEC Code of Practice* is reproduced in this book on page 189. It is also available from

http://www.itecworld.co.uk/proff_intro.html

* Contact the professional body for your professional area and obtain a code of practice. Some of the more common ones are listed here.

Aromatherapy Organisations Council (AOC) www.aoc.uk.net

Association of Reflexologists (AOR) www.aor.org.uk

British Association for Counselling and Psychotherapy (BACP) www.bac.co.uk

British Association of Beauty Therapists and Cosmetologists (BABTAC) www.babtac.com

British Association of Occupational Therapists (BAOT) www.cot.org.uk

British Complementary Medicine Association (BCMA) www.bcma.co.uk

British Reflexology Association (BRA) www.britreflex.co.uk

Chartered Society of Physiotherapy (CSP) www.csp.org.uk

Federation of Holistic Therapists (FHT) www.fht.org.uk

Guild of Complementary Practitioners www.gcpnet.com

Guild of Professional Beauty Therapists www.beautyserve.com

Independent Professional Therapists International (IPTI) www.iptiuk.com

Institute for/British General Council of Complementary Medicine (ICM/BGCCM) www.icmedicine.co.uk

International Federation of Aromatherapists (IFA) www.int-fed.aromatherapy.co.uk

The Society of Teachers of the Alexander Technique www.stat.org.uk

Institute of Sports Massage & Physical Therapy www.ismpt.ire

Professional journals

This is by no means a comprehensive list, but will help to get you started.

Aromatherapy Today Alembic Publishing

Complementary Therapies in Nursing and

Midwifery (Churchill Livingstone)

GCP Newsletter (Guild of Complementary Practitioners)

Guild News (the Journal of the Guild of Professional Therapists)

Health and Beauty Salon (Reed Business Publishing)

Health Review (Institute of Health Sciences, London)

Here's Health Magazine EMAP Publications

In Touch (British Association of Beauty Therapy and Cosmetology)

IPTI Newsletter (Independent Professional Therapists International)

Professional Beauty Magazine, London

Massage World – The Massage and Body Therapists Magazine

Massage: News, Views and Updates (Massage Therapy Institute of Great Britain)

Section 3 The environment
Health and safety
The following titles are published by the Health and Safety Executive.

Almond, E (2001) *Safety in the Salon* Thomson Learning

Croner's *A-Z guide to Health and Safety*

Health and safety regulation – a short guide HSE13

Working with Employers The Health and Safety Executive HSE35

The Health and Safety Executive and You HSE34

The Health and Safety Commission: Enforcement Policy Statement MISC030

Health and Safety Law: what you should know

Employers' Liability (Compulsory Insurance Act) 1969: a guide for employers

Workplace, Health, Safety and Welfare – a short guide for employers

St John Ambulance First-Aid Book (latest edition)

www.hse.gov.uk is the Health and Safety Executive's website

First aid
The First-Aid Manual Dorling Kindersley

First Aid at Work Health and Safety Commission

Health and Safety Executive leaflet, 'First aid at work: Your questions answered', IND(G)214L 3/97 C500

Health and Safety Executive leaflet, 'Basic advice on first aid at work' (ISBN 0 7176 1070 5)

Health and Safety Executive leaflet, 'First aid at work: Approved Code of Practice' (ISBN 0 7176 0150 0)

British Red Cross Society
9 Grosvenor Crescent
London SW1X 7EJ
Tel: 020 7235 5454
Fax: 020 7245 6315
Web: www.redcross.org.uk

St John Ambulance
27 St John's Lane
London EC1M 4BU
Tel: 020 7324 4000
Fax: 020 7324 4001
Web: www.sja.org.uk

St. Andrew's Ambulance Association
St. Andrew's House
48 Milton Street
Glasgow G4 0HR
Tel: 0141 332 4031
Fax: 0141 332 6582
Email: firstaid@staaa.demon.co.uk

Incident Contact Centre
Caerphilly Business Park
Caerphilly CF83 3GG
Tel: 0845 300 9923
Fax: 0845 300 9924

Fire safety
Fire Safety: An Employers Guide Home Office ISBN 0 11 34 1229 0

Hygiene and sterilisation
Essentials of Health and Safety at Work
Health and Safety Executive HMSO
Peberdy, W G (1988) *Sterilisation and Hygiene* Nelson Thornes
Employing staff
Employing staff – a guide to regulatory requirements DTI
Small firms: setting up in business DTI
Employing people ACAS
Rights of Access – goods, facilities, services and premises Disability Rights Commission
Race Relations Code of Practice for Employment Commission for Racial Equality

Department of Trade and Industry (DTI)
1 Victoria Street
London SW1H 0ET
Tel: 020 7215 5000
Web: www.dti.gov.uk

Advisory, Conciliation and Arbitration Service (ACAS)
Brandon House
180 Borough High Street
London SE1 1LW
Tel: 020 7210 3613 (head office)
Web: www.acas.org.uk

Stressline
The Orchard
Town Street
Horsforth
West Yorkshire LS18 5BN
Tel: 0113 258 55515

Employers/Employees Helpline
Tel: 0345 143143

Data protection and equal opportunities
Information Commissioners Office
Wycliffe House
Water Lane
Wilmslow
Cheshire SK9 5AX
Tel: 01625 545745
Fax: 01625 524510
Web: www.dataprotection.gov.uk

Equal Opportunities Commission (EOC)
Arndale House
Arndale Centre
Manchester M4 3E0
Tel: 0845 601 5901
Fax: 0845 601 5901
Web: www.eoc.org.uk

Commission for Racial Equality (CRE)
Elliot House
10–12 Allington Street
London SW1E 5EH
Tel: 020 7828 7022
Fax: 020 7630 7605
Web: www.cre.gov.uk

Disability Rights Commission (DRC)
Freepost MID 012164
Stratford-upon-Avon CV37 9BR
Tel: 0845 762 2633
Fax: 0845 762 2644

A helpful government website is:
www.disability.gov.uk

Professional membership and licensing
ITEC Professionals
4 Heathfield Terrace
London W4 4JE
Tel: 020 8994 4141
Fax: 020 8994 7880
Email: professionals@itecworld.co.uk
Web: www.itecworld.co.uk

National Care Standards Commission
St Nicholas Building
St Nicholas Street
Newcastle upon Tyne NE1 1NB
Tel: 0191 233 3660
Fax: 0191 233 3569
Email: enquiries@ncsc.gsi.gov.uk
Web: www.carestandards.org.uk
Helpline (Mon–Fri 9am–5pm) 0191 233 3556

Section 4 Business development and marketing
Peters, T (1982) *In Search of Excellence* Harper Collins